Nan Van Den Bergh
Editor

Emerging Trends for EAPs in the 21st Century

Emerging Trends for EAPs in the 21st Century has been co-published simultaneously as *Employee Assistance Quarterly*, Volume 16, Numbers 1/2 2000

Pre-Publication
REVIEWS,
COMMENTARIES,
EVALUATIONS . . .

"**A** n engineering quote says–'the best way to predict the future is to invent it.' The editor sets the right tone for a new paradigm of EAP practice, which includes client empowerment within an ecological context. The new paradigm has as its basis a general systems conceptual framework that is holistic, organic, and representative of a bio-psycho-social approach. The important message of this book is that the EAP client is the individual, the family, the organization, and community–society. Congratulations to the authors (and, Haworth Press) for a significant contribution as we move into the twenty-first century, where the homeplace and the workplace must be partners for both public health and productivity."

William L. Mermis, PhD
Professor, Human Health
Arizona State University
East Campus

Emerging Trends for EAPs in the 21st Century

Emerging Trends for EAPs in the 21st Century has been co-published simultaneously as *Employee Assistance Quarterly,* Volume 16, Numbers 1/2 2000.

The *Employee Assistance Quarterly* Monographic "Separates"

Below is a list of "separates," which in serials librarianship means a special issue simultaneously published as a special journal issue or double-issue *and* as a "separate" hardbound monograph. (This is a format which we also call a "DocuSerial.")

"Separates" are published because specialized libraries or professionals may wish to purchase a specific thematic issue by itself in a format which can be separately cataloged and shelved, as opposed to purchasing the journal on an on-going basis. Faculty members may also more easily consider a "separate" for classroom adoption.

"Separates" are carefully classified separately with the major book jobbers so that the journal tie-in can be noted on new book order slips to avoid duplicate purchasing.

You may wish to visit Haworth's website at . . .

http://www.HaworthPress.com

. . . to search our online catalog for complete tables of contents of these separates and related publications.

You may also call 1-800-HAWORTH (outside US/Canada: 607-722-5857), or Fax: 1-800-895-0582 (outside US/Canada: 607-771-0012), or e-mail at:

getinfo@haworthpressinc.com

Emerging Trends for EAPs in the 21st Century, edited by Nan Van Den Bergh, PhD, LCSW (Vol. 16, No. 1/2, 2000). *"AN EXCELLENT BOOK . . . . Relevant with respect to contemporary practice and current state of the art for EAPs. A sound disciplinary input for both program development and service delivery." (William L. Mermis, PhD, Professor of Human Health, Arizona State University)*

Employee Assistance Services in the **New South Africa,** edited by R. Paul Maiden, PhD (Vol. 14, No. 3, 1999). *Addresses the many issues affecting the development of EAP programs in the new South Africa.*

Women in the Workplace and Employee Assistance Programs: Perspectives, Innovations, and Techniques for Helping Professionals , edited by Marta Lundy PhD, LCSW, and Beverly Younger, MSW, ACSW (Vol. 9, No. 3/4, 1994). *"A valuable resource and training guide to EAP practitioners and managers alike. Most importantly, it increases the sensitivity of women's issues as they relate to the workplace." (R. Paul Maiden, PhD, Chair, Occupational Social Work, Jane Addams College of Social Work, University of Illinois at Chicago)*

Employee Assistance Programs in South Africa, edited by R. Paul Maiden, MSW (Vol. 7, No. 3, 1992). *"The first comprehensive collection of perspectives on EAPs in an industrializing third-world country." (Brian McKendrick, PhD, Professor and Head, School of Social Work, University of the Witwaterstrand, Johannesburg)*

Occupational Social Work Today, edited by Shulamith Lala Ashenberg Straussner, DSW, CEAP (Vol. 5, No. 1, 1990). *"A well-organized overview of social work practice in business . . . interesting and timely." (Journal of Clinical Psychiatry)*

Evaluation of Employee Assistance Programs, edited by Marvin D. Feit, PhD, and Michael J. Holosko, PhD (Vol. 3, No. 3/4, 1989). *"The definitive work in the field of program evaluations of EAPs. . . . A must for anyone considering planning, implementing, and most importantly, evaluating employee assistance programs." (Dr. Gerald Erickson, Professor and Director, School of Social Work, University of Windsor)*

Alcohol in Employment Settings: The Results of the WHO/ILO International Review, edited by D. Wayne Corneil, ScD (cand.) (Vol. 3, No. 2, 1988). *Valuable insights into attitudes about alcohol and the effects of its use with courses of action for educating and treating employees who need help with alcohol problems.*

EAPs and the Information Revolution: The Dark Side of Megatrends, edited by Keith McClellan and Richard E. Miller, PhD (Vol. 2, No. 2, 1987). *A serious examination of treatment methods that can be used to help working people cope with a rapidly changing economic society.*

Emerging Trends for EAPs in the 21st Century

Nan Van Den Bergh, PhD, LCSW
Editor

Emerging Trends for EAPs in the 21st Century has been co-published simultaneously as *Employee Assistance Quarterly,* Volume 16, Numbers 1/2 2000.

The Haworth Press, Inc.
New York • London • Oxford

Emerging Trends for EAPS in the 21st Century has been co-published simultaneously as *Employee Assistance Quarterly,* Volume 16, Numbers 1/2 2000.

The development, preparation, and publication of this work has been undertaken with great care. However, the publisher, employees, editors, and agents of The Haworth Press and all imprints of The Haworth Press, Inc., including The Haworth Medical Press® and Pharmaceutical Products Press®, are not responsible for any errors contained herein or for consequences that may ensue from use of materials or information contained in this work. Opinions expressed by the author(s) are not necessarily those of The Haworth Press, Inc.

The Haworth Press, Inc., 10 Alice Street, Binghamton, NY 13904-1580 USA

Cover design by Thomas J. Mayshock Jr.

Library of Congress Cataloging-in-Publication Data

Emerging trends for EAPs in the 21st century/Nan Van Den Bergh, editor.
    p. cm.
    "Co-published simultaneously as Employee assistance quarterly, volume 16, numbers 1/2 2000."
    Includes bibliographical references and index.
    ISBN 0-7890-1019-4 (alk. paper)–ISBN 0-7890-1020-8 (alk. paper)
    1. Employee assistance programs. I. Title: Emerging trends for Employee assistance programs in the 21st century. II. Van Den Bergh, Nan. III. Employee assistance quarterly.
HF5549.5.E42 E464 2000
331.25–dc21

00-046153

Dedication

This volume is humbly dedicated to all those who have felt the pain and angst of life on life's terms . . . and who have had the courage to ask for help. For all those who have struggled with an addiction, either themselves having succumbed, or those caring for an alcoholic or addict, who asked for help. To those trying to balance the demands of family life and work; to those struggling with despair and anxiety . . . and asked for help. And, for all those who have felt passion, conviction and empathy in trying to make the workplace a caring and helping environment . . . this volume is dedicated to you.

Indexing, Abstracting & Website/Internet Coverage

This section provides you with a list of major indexing & abstracting services. That is to say, each service began covering this periodical during the year noted in the right column. Most Websites which are listed below have indicated that they will either post, disseminate, compile, archive, cite or alert their own Website users with research-based content from this work. (This list is as current as the copyright date of this publication.)

Abstracting, Website/Indexing Coverage .... Year When Coverage Began

- **BUBL Information Service: An Internet-based Information Service for the UK higher education community** *<URL:http://bubl.ac.uk/>* **1995**

- **CNPIEC Reference Guide: Chinese National Directory of Foreign Periodicals** **1995**

- **EAP Abstracts Plus** **1994**

- **Family Studies Database (online and CD/ROM)** **1996**

- **FINDEX** *<www.publist.com>* **1999**

- **Human Resources Abstracts (HRA)** **1985**

- **Index to Periodical Articles Related to Law** **1985**

- **Medical Benefits** **1985**

- **NIAAA Alcohol and Alcohol Problems Science Database (ETOH)** *<http://etoh.niaaa.nih.gov>* **1991**

- **OCLC Public Affairs Information Service** *<www.pais.org>* **1985**

- **Personnel Management Abstracts** **1988**

- **Psychological Abstracts (PsycINFO)** **1986**

(continued)

- *Social Services Abstracts* <www.csa.com> **1985**

- *Social Work Abstracts* **1988**

- *Sociological Abstracts (SA)* <www.csa.com> **1985**

- *SOMED (social medicine) Database* **1985**

- *Spanish Technical Information System on Drug Abuse*
  Prevention "Sistema de Informacion Tecnica Sobre
  Prevention del Abuso de Drogas" (In Spanish)
  <http://www.idea-prevencion.com> **1999**

- *UP-TO-DATE Publications* **1996**

Special Bibliographic Notes related to special journal issues
(separates) and indexing/abstracting:

- indexing/abstracting services in this list will also cover material in any "separate" that is co-published simultaneously with Haworth's special thematic journal issue or DocuSerial. Indexing/abstracting usually covers material at the article/chapter level.
- monographic co-editions are intended for either non-subscribers or libraries which intend to purchase a second copy for their circulating collections.
- monographic co-editions are reported to all jobbers/wholesalers/approval plans. The source journal is listed as the "series" to assist the prevention of duplicate purchasing in the same manner utilized for books-in-series.
- to facilitate user/access services all indexing/abstracting services are encouraged to utilize the co-indexing entry note indicated at the bottom of the first page of each article/chapter/contribution.
- this is intended to assist a library user of any reference tool (whether print, electronic, online, or CD-ROM) to locate the monographic version if the library has purchased this version but not a subscription to the source journal.
- individual articles/chapters in any Haworth publication are also available through the Haworth Document Delivery Service (HDDS).

Emerging Trends for EAPs
in the 21st Century

CONTENTS

About the Contributors   xiii

Acknowledgments   xvii

Where Have We Been?. . . Where Are We Going?:
    Employee Assistance Practice in the 21st Century   1
    Nan Van Den Bergh

Dependent Care in the 21st Century: Broadening the Definition
    for Employee Assistance Practice   15
    Carol Hoffman

Employee Assistance and Work/Family Programs:
    Friends or Foes?   33
    Patricia A. Herlihy

EAP Services to Older Adults in the Workplace:
    A Strengths Perspective   53
    Kathleen Perkins

EAPs and Critical Incident Stress Debriefing:
    A Look Ahead   77
    David Plaggemars

An EAP Approach to Managing Organizational Downsizing   97
    Dave Worster

Organizational Development: An EAP Approach   117
    Myron Beard

Index   141

ABOUT THE EDITOR

Nan Van Den Bergh, PhD, LCSW, received her MSW from Syracuse University and doctorate from the University of Pittsburgh. As a student of labor and industrial relations in addition to social work, she was initially introduced to occupational social services through Member Assistance Programs in Pittsburgh in the late 1970's. Van Den Bergh began direct services EAP work in 1983 working in a hospital-based outpatient mental health and EAP Program. She was the Director of the University of California Staff and Faculty Counseling and Consultation Services (EAP) from 1988-1993. During that time she increased the program to include seven staff, who served 16,000 employees, offering an array of direct and indirect EAP services including wellness programs, CISD interventions, workshops, trainings and conferences for the larger Los Angeles EAP community.

At present she is faculty at Humboldt State University, the northern campus of the California State University system, and serves as an external EAP provider for several national and statewide EAP providers. Van Den Bergh has written on several topics in the EAP field including: workplace mutual aid and peer support groups, critical incident stress debriefings, workplace diversity, and gay/lesbian issues at the workplace. She is also an acknowledged author in social work, having edited two books on feminist practice, and a third on addictive disorders. Currently she serves on the Editorial Board of *Social Work Practice and the Addictions*; previously she served on the Editorial Board of *Social Work*.

ABOUT THE CONTRIBUTORS

Myron Beard, PhD, is Senior Vice President of Organizational Development for First Data Corporation, a Fortune 500 Company with 27,000 employees. He received his doctorate in Counseling Psychology from the University of North Texas. Formerly Dr. Beard was a senior consultant for RHR International Corporation, a management consulting company. Currently he is responsible for leadership development programs throughout First Data Corporation. Dr. Beard has previously been a contributor to EAP journals on the topic of organizational development.

Patricia A. Herlihy, PhD, is a psychiatric nurse clinician with a doctorate in social policy from the Florence Heller Graduate School at Brandeis University. She has over 20 years of psychiatric experience including: inpatient adult psychiatry, outpatient family therapy, adolescent substance abuse treatment, Assistant Professor in Boston University's Graduate Nursing Program, System's Manager for Digital Equipment Corporation's EAP; and, Principal Investigator for a national study associated with the Boston University Center on Work and Family.

Dr. Herlihy has presented papers at national employee assistance program conferences, as well as professional nursing and work/family program national events. Her current outside interests include organizational board leadership; and, coaching responsibilities for youth soccer programs.

Carol Hoffman, LCSW, MSW, CEAP, is a California Licensed Clinical Social Worker and has been an employee assistance professional for over twenty years. She founded and managed two employee assistance programs, at Kaiser Permanente Medical Center, S.F., CA, and subsequently at University of California at Berkeley, CA. Currently she is manager of work/life program development at UC Berkeley and co-chairs the Chancellor's Advisory Committee on Dependent Care and the Chancellor's Workgroup on Responding to Student, Faculty and Staff Deaths in the Campus Community.

Ms. Hoffman's interest in dependent care dates back to her earlier medical social work experience. Over the years she has developed elder care EAP counseling and referral services, provided training and consultation to other EAP and work/life professionals, and participated on professional EAP and work/life committees and organizations locally and nationally. With the Chancellor's Advisory Committee on Dependent Care, she authored and published Elder/Adult Dependent Caregiving by UC Berkeley Faculty and Staff, 1994, and A Guide for Balancing Work and Family, 1998.

Kathleen Perkins, DSW, received her doctorate from the University of Pennsylvania, an MSW from Portland State University and an MA in gerontology from the University of Pennsylvania. She also holds the Margaret Champagne Womack Professorship in Addictive Disorders at Louisiana State University, where she has been faculty in the school of social work for eleven years. Dr. Perkins is co-author with Carolyn Tice of the book *Mental Health Issues and Aging: Building on the Strengths of Older Persons*. Related to the strengths perspective, she has authored several other publications and has given many workshops and conference presentations on the strengths model of practice. Her current work focuses on dealing with racism in mental health and other social service delivery systems.

David Plaggemars, MSW, CEAP, ACSW, received his MSW from the University of Michigan in 1978. A Licensed Marriage and Family Therapist, he also retains credentials as Addictions Counselor and EMDR. Mr. Plaggemars has served as a past president of the Western Michigan Employee Assistance Association; and, in 1998 co-developed a mobile critical incident response team which responded to serious industrial fatalities.

Mr. Plaggemars has responded to over 200 critical incident interventions. In 1995, he successfully coordinated a multiple debriefing initiative for survivors of the United States' third most devastating school tragedy. This was a fire at Our Lady of the Angels School, whereby there were 95 fatalities. He has lectured in CISD at the University of Illinois and the University of Michigan schools of social work. Mr. Plaggemars is currently a private practice consultant designing and implementing team building and change management strategies in business and industry.

Nan Van Den Bergh, PhD, LCSW, received her MSW from Syracuse University and doctorate from the University of Pittsburgh. As a student of labor and industrial relations in addition to social work, she was initially introduced to occupational social services through Member Assistance Programs in Pittsburgh in the late 1970's. Van Den Bergh began direct services EAP work in 1983 working in a hospital-based outpatient mental health and EAP program. She was the Director of the University of California Staff and Faculty Counseling and Consultation Services (EAP) from 1988-1993. During that time she increased the program to include seven staff, who served 16,000 employees, offering an array of direct and indirect EAP services including wellness programs, CISD interventions, workshops, trainings and conferences for the larger Los Angeles EAP community.

At present she is faculty at Humboldt State University, the northern campus of the California State University system, and serves as an external EAP provider for several national and statewide EAP providers. Van Den Bergh has written on several topics in the EAP field including: workplace mutual aid and peer support groups, critical incident stress debriefings, workplace diversity, and gay/lesbian issues at the workplace. She is also an acknowledged author in social work, having edited two books on feminist practice, and a third on addictive disorders. Currently she serves on the Editorial Board of *Social Work Practice and the Addictions*; previously she served on the Editorial Board of *Social Work*.

Dave Worster, LCSW, CEAP, has served as Coordinator of Concord Hospital (New Hampshire) EAP since 1989. He holds a BS degree in education from Keene State College (New Hampshire) and master's degree in social work from the University of Connecticut. Currently Dave sits on the Employee Assistance Professionals Association Board of Directors as the Eastern Region Director. In addition, Dave has served as an Adjunct Faculty for the University of New Hampshire Department of Social Work since 1987.

Acknowledgments

It is with great appreciation that I acknowledge the help, support and guidance of Keith McClellan, Editor-in-Chief of *Employee Assistance Quarterly*. Keith has been a pioneer in the EAP field, and is responsible for the development of scholarly standards in the EAP literature. His has not been an easy task; and, there have been many struggles he has had to endure in bringing ethics of accountability and excellence to the EAP field.

Keith, you are admired and very much respected. Thank you for giving us a forum for the exchange of information, research and knowledge.

Where Have We Been? . . .
Where Are We Going?:
Employee Assistance Practice
in the 21st Century

Nan Van Den Bergh

SUMMARY. This chapter addresses changing trends within the EAP field; and, discusses the prevalence of EAPs internationally. There has been a change in focus from earlier EAPs, which were somewhat sequestered away within the organizational structure; and, with a focus most exclusively on the "troubled employee." A program model which may be more salient for the diverse employee needs of today would be a strengths-based and solution focused approach and an EAP involved in multiple aspects of an organization's work culture. *[Article copies available for a fee from The Haworth Document Delivery Service: 1-800-342-9678. E-mail address: <getinfo@haworthpressinc.com> Website: <http://www.HaworthPress.com>]*

KEYWORDS. Strengths-based, solution focused employee assistance program

It may be the case that one of the most important workplace innovations of the 20th century was the development of EAPs. Initially born from a concern with alcohol impaired employees, EAPs have grown to serve employees affected by a variety of stressors associated with working in rapidly changing workplaces, as well as the exigencies

[Haworth co-indexing entry note]: "Where Have We Been? . . . Where Are We Going?: Employee Assistance Practice in the 21st Century." Van Den Bergh, Nan. Co-published simultaneously in *Employee Assistance Quarterly* (The Haworth Press, Inc.) Vol. 16, No. 1/2, 2000, pp. 1-13; and: *Emerging Trends for EAPs in the 21st Century* (ed: Nan Van Den Bergh) The Haworth Press, Inc., 2000, pp. 1-13. Single or multiple copies of this article are available for a fee from The Haworth Document Delivery Service [1-800-342-9678, 9:00 a.m. - 5:00 p.m. (EST). E-mail address: getinfo@haworthpressinc.com].

1

associated with balancing work and family issues. This volume seeks to offer insight and pragmatic information on evolving themes for EAPs, as we move into the 21st century. In doing so, two primary themes are addressed by contributors: (a) the impact of changing workforce demography as it portends to the need for workplace sponsored services assisting caregivers and older workers; plus, (b) the development of intervention skills broader than generic assessment and referral, to help organizations manage crisis, change and evolution.

Consequently, it appears that because of the evolutionary changes in the nature of work, workers and work organizations, the core technology "troubled employee" conceptual model of EAP service delivery may need revision. It is the thesis of this author that EAP services for the 21st century may be better provided emanating from a strengths-based, empowerment and ecological model of EAPs.

Oh no, you say . . . not some New Age California counterculture, biodegradable and vegetarian notion about how to do EAP work! Hardly. To suggest that EAP may be best provided from a focus on strengths assessed from an ecological perspective is to move EA work into conformity with important trends affecting the delivery of human services over the last ten to fifteen years. Perhaps as an outcome of a confluence of multiple factors including the human rights activist movements of the 1960's and 1970's, coupled with epistemological alterations in the nature of knowledge, as well as by an increasing emphasis on holistic health, wellness and spirituality . . . a focus for human intervention has been on looking for strengths, not pathologies. Hence, in many professions and academic disciplines, new paradigms for providing help to others have emerged with varying names, such as strengths (Saleeby, 1997; Tice & Perkins, 1996), resiliencies (Fraser, 1997; Frazier, Byrne and Klein, 1995), hardiness (Kobusa, 1979) empowerment (Gutierrez, Parson & Cox, 1998) and solution-focused approaches (DeJong & Miller, 1995). The common denominator amongst these approaches is a switch in focus from problems and "troubled" individuals, to a perspective emphasizing empowerment, strengths, competencies and capabilities.

To take a focus off of trouble seems innately provocative for employee assistance endeavors, as the profession was given birth from a concern with troubled employees; primarily alcoholics who were overwhelmingly male (Trice and Schonbrunn, 1981; Steele, 1989;

Steele & Trice, 1995; Bickerton, 1990). Similarly, the core technology coined by Roman and Blum (1985) was quite specifically focused on devising an intervention technology which would be effective in training management how to confront a "troubled employee"; and, how to assess and refer such persons so as to ensure their receipt of effective treatment, and return to the workplace as productive. It is true that in the last number of years literature within the EAP profession has been challenging core technology assumptions and suggesting that the functions of employee assistance must evolve to meet the needs of a rapidly changing international world economy (Yandrick, 1994; Tisone, 1994, Lung, 1994). Evolving EAPs would include a focus on all the content areas addressed in this special edition, including child/elder/dependent care services, prevention/interventions for older workers, work/family programs, critical incident interventions, management consultation; plus, areas such as health and wellness promotion. Hence, the original three session assessment and referral paradigm to address the "troubled employee" is perhaps too parochial a focus for EA service delivery into the next century.

In addition to change in conceptualization of EAP core technology, the structure of EA programs has altered drastically from norms of the early 1970's when the first employee assistance programs were formed. For example, in 1972 there were 300 national occupational alcoholism programs, the precursors to EAPs; these were overwhelmingly internal programs. It is estimated that at present there are approximately 20,000 employee assistance programs internationally (EAPA, 1996); 80% of Fortune 500 companies have an EAP in place (EAPA, 1996); 76% of U.S. companies with 1000+ employees have an EAP and 33% of all work sites with 50+ full time employees offer EA services (Hartwell, Steele, French, Potter, Rodman & Zarkin, 1994). Using that figure to calculate access, one finds that 55.3% of the U.S. workforce has EA services available to them.

As the number of EAPs have grown, a radical shift has occurred in the venue of delivery for such services. Recent research based upon national sampling of EA programs determined that only 2.2% of work sites had an internal and external program; internal programs provided 16.7% of services with the remaining 81.1% of EA services being offered through external programs (Hartwell et al., 1994). It is assumed that approximately 15,000 of the 20,000 EAPs now extant, are external companies.

The switch from "inside" to "outside" has been most significantly affected by the impact of managed mental health and substance abuse services. Commensurate with the growth of PPOs and HMOs, has been the potential for such behavioral health care networks to offer employee assistance as a gatekeeping function for carved out mental health and chemical dependency benefits. Although seemingly a threat to the ongoing viability of EAPs, this market-based change can be reconceptualized as an opportunity for EA professionals to expand upon what they already do well. That is, in addition to supervisory training, employee orientation, management consultation, and assessment/referral services; EAPs can expand the focus of their interventions, as well as the technologies by which they do their work. It may be that offering more prevention, early intervention, and health/well-being programs, in addition to providing organizational interventions will become an important justification for EA services not being subsumed under PPOs and HMOs. Hence, EAP opportunity may lie in becoming an ecologically-oriented, strengths-based EA practitioner, able to provide such above noted services.

BECOMING AN ECOLOGICALLY-ORIENTED/ STRENGTHS-BASED PRACTITIONER

21st century EAP direct services may be better operationalized from a strengths and solution-oriented case management approach (Christensen, Todahl & Barrett, 1999; Rapp, 1998), rather than an assessment and referral model. The first step in this strengths-based approach, is to conceptualize the various systemic forces having an impact upon the employee; this is called the client's ecosystem. What constitutes, then, an ecological approach? First, and foremost, rather than seeing a client system as "troubled," one conceptualizes the individual as "challenged." An assumption exists that the challenge is transactional; that is to say, there is a lack of goodness of fit between the client and what she/he needs to be optimally productive. The client's environment, or ecosystem, includes all those systems which impact upon an employee, such as the workplace, family/personal life, health, biopsychosocial, spiritual and cultural dynamics which interact to impact an individual's ability to cope and display competence. Within an ecological model, holism is operative; and, this means that just as environmental factors affect an individual, the individual also impacts her/his environment. Hence, reciprocity becomes a focus of ecologically-based interventions. That is to say, to what extent will changes within an individual affect her environment; and, conversely, how will environmental changes affect an individual? This model does not suggest an abrogation of personal responsibility for harmful behaviors to self or others. Rather, it suggests that "moving into the solution" requires an intervention which addresses all aspects of a client's life, or ecosystem. An ecologically-oriented approach, therefore, is holistic and looks at interlocking dynamics that affect the source of a client's challenge; and, how to move toward a solution.

This conceptual model should make implicit sense for any person having worked within the EA field. We know that despite EAPs being born from occupational alcoholism concerns, the most prevalent problems addressed are not substance abuse. For example, a 1996 survey of EA professionals found that the most prevalent problems found, in descending order, were: (a) family issues (25%), (b) stress (23%), (c) depression (21%), (d) alcoholism (14%), (e) workplace/job conflict (9%) and (f) drug abuse (2%) (EAPA, 1996). These data clearly indicate that problems in living, managing one's ecosystem as it were, are the chief reasons why clients seek our help.

The question then becomes, how does one operationalize an ecological perspective into EA work and how does it inform practice? To address that question it also becomes important to incorporate components of a strengths-based and solution-focused framework into one's intervention. Operating from a strengths-based perspective also necessitates that the moniker "troubled-employee" be supplanted with a different lexicon which includes these concepts:

- empowerment
- suspension of disbelief
- dialogue and collaboration
- membership
- resilience
- healing and wellness
- synergy (DeJong & Miller, 1995; Saleeby, 1997).

Additionally, the following are principles of the strengths perspective:

- Every individual, couple, family, group, organization and community has strengths
- Trauma and abuse, illness and struggle may be injurious; but, they may also be sources of challenge and opportunity
- Assume that you don't know the upper limits of the capacity for individuals, couples, families, groups and communities to grow and change
- We best serve clients by collaborating with them
- Every environment is full of resources (Saleeby, 1997; McMillen, 1999)

Needless to say, those concepts and principles come from a different orientation than constructive confrontation with troubled employees. They mirror a more evolved and holistic perspective on human nature which has been significantly associated with the increasing diversity of our society. It is specifically because of our increasing diversity and rapidly evolving organizational and business climate that the six articles within this anthology serve as state-of-the-art descriptions in how to provide EA services in the next millennium.

The question remains, how does one implement an ecologically-focused, strengths-based approach into EAP work? Ecologically related questions might include the following:

1. Who is the client system? (the employee, the employee plus other family/social supports, the employee and coworkers/supervisors, etc.).
2. What's going on intrinsic to the client system? (Workplace performance issues; health and wellness challenges; biopsychosocial dynamics; spiritual issues, cultural factors; interactional/relational/familial concerns).
3. What's going on extrinsic to the client system? (Workplace or family dynamics such as downsizing or divorce; economic or occupational concerns such as limited jobs or blocked opportunities; institutional inequities such as racism, sexism, heterosexism; community challenges such as unemployment, violence).
4. How do the "inside" and "outside" connect? (How are factors external to the client wielding an impact on the client; how is the client affecting her/his environment?)

5. How has this client system moved through time? (How has the client addressed challenges previously?) (Adapted from Miley, O'Melia & DuBois, 1998, p. 46).

As is suggested by the above discussion, incorporating a strengths-based and solution-focused approach along with an ecological perspective, requires that an EA practitioner operate from the assumption that there are inherent strengths within the client and her/his environment which can be used to address the challenge; and, that failure is impossible. Specifically, assessing for strengths includes visioning three time periods:

- today
- yesterday
- tomorrow

As for the present, the EA practitioner needs to determine what personal, interpersonal and structural strengths exist within the client and her/his ecosystem which can be mobilized and deployed to resolve the client's challenge. For example, let us assume a female client comes to the EAP, concerned about an abusive, interpersonal relationship. You determine she has been battered, the batterer abuses alcohol and drugs, she fears for her safety and her kids'. Despite the abuse, this client is reluctant to consider leaving the perpetrator as she does not believe that she could cope as a single parent. The immediate strengths to be ascertained from that opening scenario are:

- willingness to ask for help
- concern for her children's welfare and her partner's wellbeing
- acknowledgment of her partner's substance abuse problem

A strengths-based practitioner would validate the client's concerns, express empathy and support, acknowledge strengths she is demonstrating by asking for help; and, work with the client in determining a safety plan. Solution-focused questions the EA professional might ask which would be empowering; hence, potentially helpful in motivating the client to take action steps could include:

- "You have really been facing up to this challenge. How have you been doing that?"

- "You must be amazingly resilient to keep going on under these circumstances. Where do you find the strength to go on?"

Having located strengths while discussing challenges, an EA practitioner would then assess what a client has attempted previously in terms of efforts to deal with her domestic violence challenge. Again, by searching for client coping mechanisms and resiliencies an EA practitioner might ask the following questions:

- "So, how have you handled this in the past?"
- "What has worked, even for a little while?"

An EA practitioner might discover from this approach that the client is abstinent from drugs and alcohol, having previously abused them; and, she has family and friends close by, who are part of her social support system. You might also discover that she has provided for herself and her children previously, prior to becoming involved with her current partner. Consequently, an EA professional would underscore her coping mechanisms of sobriety, capacity to earn a living and connections to caring persons as resources available to her, in the present, which she can use in resolving her challenge.

In order to move into the solution, a strengths-based practitioner helps the client focus on exceptions to when a problem occurs; and, what would constitute incremental steps in moving forward. Questions which would facilitate a solutions-focused, strengths-based approach in this direction might include:

- "What is happening on those days when your partner isn't abusive?"
- "What is the first thing you will notice when things are getting better? Does that ever happen now?"
- "You mentioned a period of time when all was well in your relationship and family. Could we talk about what was going on then?"

This discussion has provided a framework for reconceptualizing EAP assessment and referral from a focus on the "troubled employee" to a strengths-oriented, solution-focused and ecologically-based perspective. This framework could be considered particularly useful for the significant percentage of EA clients who present with family, stress and mental health concerns. Research has documented that subjects associated with "family difficulties," such as dependent care, elder care, etc. will remain the highest priority client demand, as we move into the millennium (Jankowski, 1989). An associated theme is the increasing "greying" of the workforce; and, the increased number of older workers needing retirement-related services. This increasingly "greying" workforce, combined with the 1990's labor force influx of women and ethnic minorities, means that there needs to be workplace-based services which offer resources on addressing employee caregiving and caretaking needs. This exigency may paradoxically harken the development of a new social contract, and a renaissance in community-building at the workplace.

A NEW SOCIAL CONTRACT: COMMUNITY AT THE WORKPLACE

There are significant historical connections between caring, community and the workplace. First, it bears mention that the industrialized workplace of the 19th century was held responsible for the dissolution of the capacity for innate caring systems, such as families and kinship networks, to provide for societal members. More agriculturally-oriented societies had networks of mutual aid and peer support undergirded by an ethic of concern for collective welfare and caring. Nineteenth century sociologist Max Weber named such societies *gemein-schaft*. However, with increasing industrialization, individuals became isolated from caring networks as they moved to cities to find jobs. With typical social supports lacking, individuals became isolated, disconnected, alienated; Weber named this kind of societal milieu *gesellschaft* (Weber, 1958). Another 19th century sociologist Emile Durkheim (1951) noted an increased suicide prevalence in the burgeoning industrialized *gesellschaft* societal context, for which he coined the term anomie. Conditions of societal anomie, then, were the seedbed for individual's suicide.

The adage that history repeats itself seems unfortunately true, if one reflects on societal conditions at the turn of the millennium. Are not ever increasing addiction prevalence and violence rates indicators of a kind of societal suicide? And, commensurately, there was an increase in suicide rates at the end of the 20th century; particularly amongst youths. We are in many ways, at present, a *gesellschaft*-affected society; and, feelings of anomie, dissatisfaction, disappointment, disillusionment and disconnection impact the workplace. As Worster indicates, in his article, the former workplace social contract between employer and employee has waned. No longer do employees believe they will have lifetime employment with a firm; this phenomenon is as true for professional and managerial employees as it is for pink and blue collar workers. Not even EA professionals are immune from being "right sized." In a related vein, Beard notes that being vulnerable to downsizing is a phenomenon that impacts organizational and business leaders as well as middle management and rank and file employees. The need for rapid responses to changing economic, market and business climate factors causes executives to have to deal with ambiguity as well as uncertainty. Such an organizational ecology becomes a context for organizational development interventions. And, Plaggemars' chapter reminds us that experiencing crisis and trauma at the workplace has become so commonplace, that EA professionals need to be adept in applying critical stress debriefing technologies.

So, what does all of this mean for EA professionals in the millennium; and, how do the two themes of caring and community converge at the workplace? In essence, the workplace needs to become a more *gemeinschaft* environment, one that acknowledges the following fact: the overwhelming majority of employees have caretaking responsibilities. Hence, provision of services, benefits, policies, and programs which address those *gemeinschaft* needs are critical in order to have a workplace ecology which allows employees to be optimally productive. Paradoxically, the workplace may serve as the optimal venue for the renaissance of caring communities.

So, what would these caring communities look like; and, what would be the role of employee assistance professionals in helping to operationalize such a workplace culture evolution/revolution? First, as Hoffman and Herlihy indicate, employees need to be seen as individuals with family needs; EAPs must be facilitators of "family friendly" services. In that regards, there needs to be an expanded definition of what constitutes family to also include persons economically dependent upon one another (although not married) and to extended family or "family of choice." Hence, the definition of "dependent" must be reconceptualized to be more flexible, so as to meld with a more realistic and enlightened definition of persons who are family, to each other.

Secondly, as Perkins underscores, by using a strengths-based approach to EAP services, employee competencies are emphasized, rather that pathologies; this allows for synergy, rather than remediation and rehabilitation. That is to say, employees may be better able to see their competencies and how they can be used to not only help themselves, but those around them. Hence, the potential for networking, establishing mutual aid and peer support opportunities, and other community-building activities might organically arise within a strengths-based workplace environment. Since a strengths-based model implies engaging in dialogue and collaboration, rather than constructive confrontation, the workplace could become a self-empowering venue for personal and collective wellbeing.

A family and strengths-based approach also undergirds the applicability of offering critical incident stress debriefings, as is noted by Plaggemars. Employees experience the same kind of feelings of loss and stress when experiencing work-associated crises (such as being laid off) as if they had gotten divorced. Hence, providing CISD interventions empowers employees by encouraging their emotional ventilation and participation in healthy self-care activities.

As mentioned previously, Worster notes grave concern that the former sense of social contract between employee and employer, built on mutual loyalty, has waned. Because employees may see themselves as expendable commodities, there could be a commensurate decline in commitment to one's job; and, productivity. He notes that EA professionals could be the harbingers of change for workplace community development by: (a) advocating for humane human resource policies which engender feelings of employee safety, (b) forming natural alliances with other organizational entities concerned with "human capital," (c) promoting open organizational communication and collaborative decision making and (d) supporting growth-oriented opportunities for employee education and development.

Beard reminds us that organizational change brings needs for help to business leaders in managing those changes. A strengths-based ecological approach is the most effective method for assisting with that kind of organizational development activity. By considering the needs of the organization pursuant to a leader's qualities, in conjunction with a manager's intrinsic strengths and competencies, OD consultant coaching can lead to an empowered executive and workplace as a result.

AS WE MOVE INTO THE MILLENNIUM . . .

As one of the single most important innovations of the 20th century workplace, EAPs afforded an opportunity for employees to get assistance for work or personal problems affecting their productivity. Albeit needing to be "troubled," employee assistance programs have clearly benefitted millions of American workers.

To be most relevant for the millennium, employee assistance needs to be delivered through a strengths-based, solution-focused, empowerment-oriented ecological model that acknowledges the interdependent relationships between employees and their work organizations. Family-friendly services delivered within a workplace community undergirded by a covenant of caring, may be the best metaphor for EAP service delivery in the millennium. By ensuring that employee wellbeing needs are acknowledged and assisted, we may all become a bit more connected to one another; and our common welfare advanced. To that end, an empowered workplace may be the most optimally productive one, for the millennium.

REFERENCES

Bickerton, R. (1990). Employee assistance: A history in progress. *EAP Digest*. Nov/Dec. 34-42, 83-84.

Christensen, D., Todahl, J. & Barrett, W. (1999) *Solution-Based Casework: An Introduction to Clinical and Case Management Skills in Casework Practice*. New York: Aldine De Gruyter.

DeJong, P. & Miller, S.D. (1995). How to interview for client strengths. *Social Work. 40.* 729-736.

Durkheim, E. (1951). *Suicide*. New York: Free Press.

Employee Assistance Professionals Association. (1996). Employee Assistance Backgrounder. Arlington, VA: EAPA.

Fraser, M.W. (Ed.) (1997). *Risk and Resilience in Childhood: An Ecological Perspective*. November 14, 1999, Washington. D.C.: NASW Press.

Frazier, P.A., Byrne, C. & Klein, C. (1995). Resilience among sexual assault survivors. Poster session presented at the annual meeting of the American Psychological Association. New York.

Gutierrez, L.M., Parsons, R.J. & Cox, E.O. (Eds.). (1998). *Empowerment in Social Work Practice: A Sourcebook*. Pacific Grove, CA: Brooks/Cole.

Hartwell, T., Steele, P., French, M., Potter, F., Rodman, N. & Zarkin, G. (1994). Prevalence, cost, and characteristics of EAPs in the United States. Research Triangle Institute, North Carolina (unpublished).

Jankowski, J., Holtgraves, M. & Gerstein, L. (1989). A systematic perspective on work and family units. In E. Goldsmith (Ed). *Work and Family, Theory, Research and Applications*. Woodland Hills, CA: Sage Publications.

Kobusa, S.C. (1979). Stressful life events, personality and health: An inquiry into hardiness. *Journal of Personality and Social Psychology. 37*. 1-11.

Lung, S. (1994). EAPs "What's Next?" *EAPA Exchange*. February. 12-13.

Miley, K., O'Melia, M., DuBois, B. (1998). *Generalist Social Work Practice: An Empowering Approach*. Boston: Allyn & Bacon.

McMillen, J. (1999). Better for it: How people benefit from adversity. *Social Work. 44* (5). 455-469.

Rapp, C. (1998). *The Strengths model*. NY: Oxford University Press.

Roman, P. & Blum, T. (1985). The core technology of employee assistance programs. *Almacan*. March. 8-9, 16, 18-19.

Saleeby, D. (Ed.) (1997). *The Strengths Perspective in Social Work Practice*. (2nd. Ed.) New York: Longman.

Steele, P. (1989). A history of job-based alcoholism programs: 1955-1972. *Journal of Drug Issues. 19* (4). 511-532.

Steele, P. & Trice, H. (1995). A history of job-based alcoholism programs: 1972-1980. *Journal of Drug Issues 25* (2) 397-422.

Tice, C. & Perkins, K. (1996). *Mental Health Issues and Aging: Building on the Strengths of Older Workers*. Pacific Grove, CA: Brooks/Cole Publishing Co.

Tisone, C. (1994). Just another burning issue. *EAPA Exchange*. February. 11.

Trice, H. & Schonbrunn, M. (1981). A history of job-based alcoholism programs: 1900-1955. *Journal of Drug Issues*. Spring. 171-198.

Weber, M. (1958). *The Protestant Ethic and the Spirit of Capitalism*. New York: Charles Scribner & Sons.

Yandrick, R. (1994). Has the core technology become an anachronism? *EAPA Exchange*. February. 6-9.

Dependent Care in the 21st Century: Broadening the Definition for Employee Assistance Practice

Carol Hoffman

SUMMARY. This chapter suggests that a significant percentage of the workforce, primarily female, is increasingly required to manage concerns with providing caregiving to family members, which can be a drain on their workplace productivity. The definition of dependent care is broadened to include not only child care; but, elder care and caregiving for an employee's significant others who may be affected by illness or a debilitating health condition. *[Article copies available for a fee from The Haworth Document Delivery Service: 1-800-342-9678. E-mail address: <getinfo@ haworthpressinc.com> Website: <http://www.HaworthPress.com>]*

KEYWORDS. Dependent care, elder care, family leave

A DEFINITION OF DEPENDENT CARE

Not long ago, when people talked about dependent care they were almost always referring to the care of minor children. That definition is changing. Shifting demographics and family structures, longer life expectancy, life-prolonging medical interventions, increasing multi-

The author wishes to thank Professor Andrew E. Scharlach, PhD, Kleiner Professor of Aging, School of Social Welfare, University of California, Berkeley, for his generosity in sharing his expertise through his research studies and writings.

[Haworth co-indexing entry note]: "Dependent Care in the 21st Century: Broadening the Definition for Employee Assistance Practice." Hoffman, Carol. Co-published simultaneously in *Employee Assistance Quarterly* (The Haworth Press, Inc.) Vol. 16, No. 1/2, 2000, pp. 15-32; and: *Emerging Trends for EAPs in the 21st Century* (ed: Nan Van Den Bergh) The Haworth Press, Inc., 2000, pp. 15-32. Single or multiple copies of this article are available for a fee from The Haworth Document Delivery Service [1-800-342-9678, 9:00 a.m. - 5:00 p.m. (EST). E-mail address: getinfo@haworthpressinc.com].

culturalism and other changes have forced us to re-examine our definitions of the caregiver and the dependent. These changes raise new questions for employee assistance providers, who must address issues related to care not only of the employee's minor children, but also of their aging parents and their ill and disabled partners and other dependents.

These changes require a shift from the once common definition of dependency based on age or on medical diagnosis to a broader definition that takes into account an overall evaluation of functional capacity and alternative resources for care. This shift has been slow to come about because, whereas dependency once focused on birthing and raising children, increasingly, dependency must focus on issues we are less comfortable with such as aging, illness, disability and death. In addition, changes in the delivery of medical care and rising health care costs mean that those with inadequate insurance coverage and those who used to receive care in hospitals and skilled nursing facilities increasingly are cared for in the home. Consequently, we must re-conceptualize dependency from a divided view that focuses on two ends of the life spectrum to a uniting view that brings together the common issues and problems associated with caring for a dependent other, whatever the cause for dependency.

Changing demographics are causing the emergence of new groups of dependent care providers. Divorces and remarriages, adoptions, geographic separations and single parenthood all contribute to a growing field of potential dependents. Even a distant relative can become a dependent if s/he is suddenly disabled and there is no closer relative available to provide care. As many people are starting families at older ages, a "sandwich generation" of young to middle-age adults is bearing increasing responsibility both for their minor children and for their aging parents. Others are caring for grandchildren, as their own children give birth at younger ages or are otherwise ill prepared to care for a child. An expanded definition of dependents must include in-laws, ex-spouses and their families, foster relatives, domestic partners, various relatives and friends.

As the definition of dependent care broadens, so does the range of responsibilities associated with caring for a dependent. Limited health coverage means that relatives often must provide care that is not considered medically skilled. People with serious illnesses or those dying who used to receive care in hospitals are increasingly cared for at home. Improvements in life-sustaining treatments mean that people live longer, though often with treatments and functional limitations as a result of illnesses and disabilities that once were expected to result in certain and rapid death.

At this time, child and elder care remain the most common forms of dependent care. Both forms of care refer to providing for individuals who must rely on others for needs associated with transportation, food, clothing, shelter, education, health care and other essentials. For children, age alone is reason for this reliance on others. Contrary to popular thinking, age is not the reason for dependence on others in the misnamed "elder care." The broader concept of dependent care includes caregiving individuals who have one or more diseases or disabilities that inhibit their independent functioning. For example, in addition to a disabled or ill elder, an employee may need to provide care for a spouse with breast cancer, a domestic partner with AIDS, a child with leukemia, a grandchild born to a drug-addicted daughter, a parent with heart disease, an uncle who is mentally retarded or an adult relative disabled in an accident. A new definition of the dependent must take into account all these circumstances, and many others. Consequently, a dependent is a person of any age whose impairments in functional abilities require a care provider to offer one or more forms of assistance on a more than one time basis.

Increasingly, dependent care has become an important workplace issue, and an inclusive definition of dependent care is critical to effective employer response. More than 70% of women age 25-54 are in the civilian workforce (Green and Epstein 1988). By the year 2000, 80% of women age 25-64 will be in the labor force, with the greatest growth among women age 45-54, who are most likely to have responsibility for aging family members (Green and Epstein, 1988). While men also care for dependents and likewise require benefits and assistance, women continue to bear most of the burden of responsibility for care of children, elderly and other dependent family members.

Dependent care benefits must take into account care for the caregiver as well as for the dependent. Caregivers need support and assistance themselves if they are to continue to carry the double burden of working and caring for dependent children, parents, partners, relatives and others. Parents need not only child care, but assistance in parenting. Elder care providers need information relative to a variety of topics such as adaptive/maladaptive changes associated with the aging pro-

cess, health and medical information, financial and social service resources, etc. Equally important is the provision of information about
mutual aid and peer support groups for caregivers. Clearly, dependent
care service delivery systems need to be associated with health care
delivery. When, and if, the health care system is redesigned nationally,
careful attention must be paid to the issues of caregiving and dependency, not just acute medical care.

SCOPE OF THE PROBLEM

Perhaps the fastest growing population of dependents is 65 years of
age and older, due to age associated chronic illnesses and disabilities.
As Friedman predicted, elder care has become the "emerging employee benefit of the 1990's" (Friedman, 1986). Eighty percent of
older persons eventually experience one or more chronic health problems (AARP, 1987, p. 13). The U.S. population of persons 65 years of
age and older grew from 3.1 million in 1900 to 33.2 million in 1994
(US Census Bureau, 1995). The number of elderly individuals has
doubled since 1960, and it is expected to more than double again by
2050 to include 80 million elderly individuals, or more than 20% of
the total U.S. population (US Census Bureau, 1995). People 85 years
and over make up the fastest growing segment of American society;
more than half of these individuals require assistance with day to day
activities (US Senate Special Committee on Aging, 1986).

A U.S. Senate Special Commission on Aging found that most
elder care is provided by family members. Working caregivers represent two thirds of all elder care providers (National Alliance for
Caregiving & AARP, 1997). Among female employees over the age
of 30, greater numbers assist elderly relatives than care for young
children (The Travelers, 1985). A *Fortune* (1989) survey showed that
elder care responsibilities interfered with job responsibilities for 77%
of caregiving employees sampled. Many caregivers have more than
one dependent simultaneously, i.e., caring for an elderly aunt plus an
elderly parent, or caring for young children, teenagers, and a grand-
parent.

A study at the University of California, Berkeley found that more
than one-quarter (27%) of respondents were currently providing assistance to an adult (over 18 years old) ill or disabled family member or
friend (Scharlach and Fredriksen 1992). Many other workplace depen-

dent care studies have found an employee caregiving prevalence rate of 20%-30%; sometimes the percent of employee caregivers has been as high as 40% (Health Action Forum 1989; Wagner et al. 1988). In the UC Berkeley study, 21.5% of faculty and staff over 30 years of age identified themselves as caregivers. Nearly two-thirds (63%) said they were currently caring for a disabled, adult family member or friend, had done so in the past five years, or expected to do so in the next five years. The majority of employee care recipients were elderly and for 50% of caregiver employees, the care recipient was a parent. Caregivers were older than survey respondents in general, but 26% were under the age of 40. Additional findings of this study indicated that three of five respondents currently assisting an ill or disabled individual were women (Scharlach and Fredriksen 1992).

DEMANDS AND STRESSORS FACED BY EMPLOYEES WITH DEPENDENT CARE RESPONSIBILITIES

Employees share a number of demands and stressors related to caregiving, no matter who is the subject of care. However, specific dependent populations and individual circumstances often contribute to additional challenges. Dependent care must be reframed from a child and aging parent issue to encompass developmental issues related to health and illness throughout the life cycle. Increasingly, issues of dependency arise throughout the lifespan as we face illnesses, such as cancer, that may bring about early and untimely disability and death. Numbers of individuals of all ages are affected by drug dependency, violence, cancer, heart disease and developmental disabilities. Nearly every working adult will encounter major life events that portend implications for dependent care during their working years. These might include birthing and/or parenting minor children, divorce and forming of new family configurations, accidents, illness and death.

Most commonly, the greatest demands upon the caregiver relate to the provision of time and money to the person requiring care. Caregivers provide direct financial assistance averaging about $150 per month; however, aid can be equivalent to $1000 per month, or more, for an older dependent in a nursing home (Scharlach 1988; Scharlach and Fredriksen 1992). There are employees who have double or triple the expenditures noted above since approximately 25% of employees with dependent care responsibilities provide assistance to two or more elderly persons (Scharlach and Fredriksen 1992).

In addition to the financial burden, employed caregivers provide just as many hours of care as caregivers who are not employed (Brody et al. 1983; Brody and Schoonover 1986; Sherman et al. 1982; Soldo and Myllyluoma 1983). These workers must sacrifice personal time, sleep, social activities and other family obligations. Costs accrue for caregiving employees from the provision of financial and time resources, as noted previously.

In terms of stressors employee caregivers experience, a Kaiser Permanente study in California showed that caregivers are more likely to suffer headaches, backaches and other stress-related problems than non-caregivers (Scharlach, Midanik et al. 1992). Women and those earning lower than average wages show higher levels of stress and anxiety when they must provide dependent care, then do men and individuals with higher salaries (*Fortune* 1989). Caregiver stress is especially acute in those caring for dependents who are mentally ill or have cognitive impairments. Such dependents may yell at a caregiver or become agitated, disruptive or demanding. Their caregivers may go to work drained by those caregiving responsibilities while experiencing additional demands and stress on the job. Research has validated that employees caring for older dependents have greater job stress and work-family conflicts than other employees (Neal et al. 1987; Scharlach and Boyd 1989).

Clearly, dependent caregivers face a variety of problems which emanate from the confluence of work and family demands. Consequently, because of demands and stressors faced by employed caregivers in the variety of roles they play, services to assist them must address their needs for emotional support, money, time, information and additional helping resources.

THE IMPACT OF DEPENDENT CARE RESPONSIBILITIES ON JOB PERFORMANCE AND ON THE WORKPLACE

Care of dependents has a dynamic impact on employees and on the workplace. A caregiver may need to respond to unanticipated events with sudden time off from work, not knowing the duration of time needed. Employees may need to take time off when a dependent's attendant is sick or no longer available. Additionally, s/he may need to travel to care for a relative, or may have to quickly obtain information about medical treatments or coverage for health care expenses. Additionally, caregivers may need time off in order to recuperate from caregiving and to acquire needed supports.

Employees caring for a dependent may suffer poor concentration, exhaustion, loss of appetite, increased illness, stress and other problems. As a result of their dual responsibilities, their employment records may be marked by high rates of absenteeism, including unplanned absences, frequent tardiness and decreased productivity. This can limit the employee's opportunities for promotion and career development. Left unchecked, these problems can generalize to decreased morale and lowered productivity in the workplace, and can result in increased costs in impaired job performance, turnover, hiring and retraining.

The average caregiving employee misses three to five hours of work each month as a direct result of elder care responsibilities, with some missing considerably more (Scharlach and Boyd 1989; Scharlach and Fredriksen 1992). In the *Fortune* (1989) survey previously mentioned, 60% of corporate executives reported specific work-related problems caused by elder care responsibilities, including stress, unscheduled days off, late arrivals, early departures, excessive use of telephone and absenteeism. Other effects might include marital problems, loss of vacation time and early retirement to fulfill caregiving responsibilities. The National Alliance for Caregiving and AARP (1997) study reports that one fifth of all caregivers ever employed while caregiving gave up work either temporarily or permanently. Chronic fatigue, headache, weight changes and anxiety may all affect job performance (Creedon 1987).

In the 1992 UC Berkeley study mentioned previously (Scharlach and Fredriksen, 1992) fully 80% of caregivers reported interference with work as a result of their dependent care responsibilities. Some felt that they might need to quit their jobs in order to continue to provide care. More than one-third of respondents reported taking off at least one day of work, with pay, in the past six months in order to provide dependent care; additionally, more than 40% used their vacation time for caregiving.

THE FEDERAL FAMILY AND MEDICAL LEAVE ACT OF 1993

This legislation requires covered employers to provide up to twelve weeks of leave per year for an employee's serious illness, the birth or adoption of a child, or caring for a sick spouse, child, or parent. This act, while a milestone towards recognizing the impact of family and employee illness and childbearing on an employee, is still limited in meeting employee dependent care needs. The twelve weeks time frame is often insufficient for addressing many acute as well as chronic health situations. The specific designation of who is covered by this legislative protection does not include domestic partners, parents-in-law, siblings, other family members and step-family relationships. However, a major advantage of the FMLA is the continuation of health benefits for the employee during the leave period. Prior to the FMLA, most leaves of absence involved discontinuation of health benefits which prevented many employees from taking leaves for which they otherwise were qualified. The hope is that many states and employers will take the spirit of the FMLA and improve on it; and, if they haven't done so already, to offer longer durations of leave and extension of the types of covered dependents (i.e., for domestic partners, siblings, grandparents).

DEPENDENT CARE
AND THE EMPLOYEE ASSISTANCE PROGRAM (EAP)

Presenting Problems Experienced by Caregiving Employees

Because dependent care responsibilities affect the work performance of the caregiver and her/his co-workers, issues related to dependent care are well suited for EAP intervention. Issues related to caring for a dependent are similar to other issues commonly addressed in employee assistance programs: bereavement, depression, stress-related problems such as insomnia or headaches, alcohol and drug use, and a host of other problems that can affect productivity and performance in the workplace, if unchecked. While EAP programs traditionally have responded to family issues, they have yet to establish a consistent programmatic response to dependent care, or even a common definition of "family."

Nearly all caregiving employees (90%) in the 1992 University of California at Berkeley study previously mentioned (Scharlach and Fredriksen 1992) reported experiencing some level of emotional strain related to their caregiving activities; two-thirds reported physical strain. The UC study found that the types of assistance caregivers most often provided to dependents include emotional reassurance, transportation, cooking, laundry, housecleaning and home maintenance, arranging and monitoring assistance provided by others, and managing the dependent's finances. A large portion of caregivers (80%) also provided direct financial assistance.

A survey of 33 companies in Portland, Oregon (Neal et al. 1987) found that employees with elder care responsibilities were more likely than other employees to experience stress related to health, finances, family relationships, family health and work. People caring for dependents with Alzheimer's disease used alcohol more frequently and had four to ten times the incidence of depression than the community as a whole (Walsh et al. 1991). Additionally, they used prescription drugs for depression, anxiety and insomnia two to three times more often than the community at large (George and Gwyther 1986). Caring for elderly relatives has been shown to be associated with increased rates of depression, somatic symptoms, increased psychotropic medication use and other stress-related physical and mental health problems. Mental health sequelae may be especially prevalent among the more than 40% of elder caregivers who also are employed full time (AARP & The Travelers Foundation 1988; Stone et al. 1987).

Dependent Care-Sensitive EAP Assessment and Referral

Appropriate EAP interventions for caregivers include assessment, resource referral, counseling, support groups, educational presentations, video programs, and written information. Caregivers may need practical help learning to deal with a relative's illness, dementia, unresponsiveness, dependency, hostility and/or physical and emotional changes. They may need assistance navigating the network of resources in the community, finding a nursing home or similar residential placement, as well as securing legal help. For example, an EAP client presented with a plan of placing a mother in a convalescent hospital. He had done the necessary research to find a listing of facilities and was seeking advice as to which facility had the best reputation. Through the EAP assessment process, it was determined that the level of care that his parent required was not the level he had identified and researched. The employee had experienced confusion in deciphering differences in caregiving and housing options; such a lack of clarity about the appropriate resource to use is common. This is caused, in part, by variation and inconsistency in terms used to describe differing types of housing and out-of-home care by service providers.

In-person assessment of the caregiver's and the recipient's needs is vital to making a comprehensive plan. As an example, a client sought EAP services when in crisis, urgently requesting legal information regarding her mother. The employee's parent had experienced a serious medical condition that significantly impaired her ability to function as she had previously. This EAP client, concerned about sibling and parental relationships, felt that an immediate and decisive action was indicated. Though the employee's need to address legal and caregiving problems was appropriate, the situation was not really a crisis. The employee's perception of being in crisis seemed to be based on experiencing uncomfortable feelings associated with the change in roles with her mother, the accompanying losses, and the need to take action. The EAP professional was able to help the employee address her feelings and to slow down the pace at which she was embarking on the long road of caregiving.

EAP providers must be attuned to identifying caregiving as a primary stressor when a client presents symptoms associated with caregiving. Clients, who may have eased gradually into a caregiving role over time, or who may have been socialized to believe they ought to provide care to dependents without complaint, can be educated to recognize caregiving as a potential source of stress. For example, an EAP client who requested services because of relationship difficulties was actually experiencing stress due to a parent moving into her home for dependent care, simultaneous with her son leaving home to go to college. As both of these moves had been perceived by the employee as normal life events, the EAP client had not viewed them as problems that could negatively affect her. The client's perception of experiencing a relationship problem could best be addressed by examining the many shifting roles and responsibilities the employee was experiencing, as a result of changing family dynamics.

To be of optimal assistance to employees experiencing caregiving stresses, an EAP needs to be not only broad-brush in scope, as opposed to the more traditional occupational alcoholism program, but also able to promote its elder care services. This will allow those employees who identify their primary problem as related to dependent care, or some other problem, to seek out EAP services. For example, many individuals also have substance abuse problems and may see their chemical dependency as a secondary problem, or not as a problem at all. These individuals will never seek out the EAP for help if it is defined only as a resource for drug and alcohol abuse. The same is true for caregivers of adult dependents.

BEYOND CARING FOR THE INDIVIDUAL CAREGIVER

In addition to helping individual employees identify and seek solutions to their problems as caregivers, the EAP can be instrumental in sensitizing supervisory, management and employee peers to dependent care responsibilities and needs by implementing a variety of direct and indirect service interventions.

Direct Service Interventions

As it pertains to direct services other than EAP assessment and referral, letting caregivers know that they are not alone in shouldering dependent care responsibilities, can help break the sense of isolation that frequently accompanies trying to balance caring for another, with addressing one's own needs. Bringing caregivers together through mutual aid and peer support groups, facilitated by EAP staff, can mobilize employee self-help efforts potentially useful in dealing with the dependent care challenges which they face.

Dependent care support groups organized and facilitated by EAP professionals will be most effective if they are of short term duration, so as not to be an additional time constraint for overburdened caregivers. An ongoing time commitment, even if during a lunch hour, could be a burden for a caregiver who is already struggling with the time demands of caregiving and work. Logistics related to group process for such a mutual aid endeavor might include open membership, a time-delimited number of sessions (for example, four, with the option of continuation), and not requiring weekly attendance. In terms of group content, participants would be encouraged to talk about their dependent care responsibilities and the specific challenges or difficulties that they have been experiencing, given their multiple roles. Themes can be discussed as they emerge from the initial disclosure of individuals' situations, e.g., changing roles with parents, dealing with the medical establishment, planning for the holidays, etc.

Another kind of mutual aid network which could be facilitated by

EAP staff would include establishing an e-mail chatline for employees with dependent care responsibilities. Although there has not yet been sufficient experience to measure the effectiveness of electronic communication to meet the emotional needs of caregivers, the ease of communication through such a peer support network has compelling possibilities.

Indirect Services

In terms of indirect services, if an organization does not have a specific work and family life program (separate from an EAP), employee assistance staff could initiate a workplace committee to identify employee caregiver needs and to investigate the implementation of such a program. Additionally, an EAP can offer supervisory training or facilitate workshops on dependent care for departments where employees have been affected by caregiving responsibilities. In a related vein, the EAP can host learn-at-lunch seminars, workshops, forums, and caregiver fairs on dependent care subjects. Other venues for EAP dependent care advocacy include participating in human resources' policy and benefits development, pursuant to employee caregivers, as well as being involved with joint employer-community dependent care resource development.

By participating in company-wide efforts to address issues related to dependent care, EAP staff can advocate for the institutionalization of policies which are helpful for employees with dependent care responsibilities. There are innumerable policies/programs which can be helpful to employees engaged in dependent care including: (a) part-time and flexible work schedules, (b) job sharing, (c) long term care insurance, (d) telecommuting, (e) working from home, (f) bereavement leave, (g) respite care, (h) brokering direct caregiving services, (i) expanded health and life insurance options for long term conditions, (j) financial assistance, (k) 403b plans and (l) omnibus brokering assistance in accessing community resources. In the University of California, Berkeley dependent care study mentioned previously (Scharlach and Fredriksen 1992), employees identified leave without loss of benefits, help in locating services in the community, long-term care insurance, the ability to adjust their work schedules, and the ability to use all of their sick leave to care for a family member, as the most desirable additional benefits, policies and services. Many of these have subsequently been developed to address these needs.

One of the most influential things an employee assistance professional can do is to broach dependent care needs within organizational discussions related to potential changes in human resource policies and benefits. Ostensibly minor changes in the way "covered conditions or employees" is defined in employee benefit policies may present a significant opportunity to receive dependent care assistance for employed caregivers.

As has been eluded to by the above, EAPs may be critically important in giving voice to dependent care as a reality which impacts the wellbeing and productivity of employees. For example, an EAP could be instrumental in helping a company to define dependent care as a workplace issue by promoting survey research undertaken to describe employee dependent care needs, to be used in crafting responsive employee dependent care benefits. EAP staff could also influence organizational policy makers to redefine family to be a more inclusive concept than the traditional nuclear family model. For example, family could be defined as adults and dependents who are financially interdependent and/or who have significant caregiving responsibilities to each other. The establishment of a more inclusive definition of policy should be extended not only for EAP program eligibility, but also for other family-defined policies and benefits. The employer who acknowledges and assists employees with the stresses of life events will be rewarded with improved productivity, loyalty and employee retention, which can result in cost savings that more than pay for any expenditures related to providing this assistance.

An elaboration of some indirect service activities, mentioned previously, which could be undertaken at the workplace to engender consciousness-raising about employee dependent care needs include activities such as forums, speakouts, or caregiver fairs. Such events publicly highlight dependent care issues while also providing information and resources to caregivers. As an example, if an organization had undertaken a needs assessment related to the dependent care needs of its employees, an open forum could then be held to review the research results. At such an event not only would the survey results be shared along with employer recommendations based on the study, feedback and suggestions from employees would also be elicited.

Another dependent care visibility event, for example, would be showing a documentary film addressing the challenges an employee faced through caregiving for a parent with Alzheimer's disease. If such an event was cosponsored by several organizational departments such as human resources, EAP, or occupational health, both awareness of the issue and information about resources would be promoted.

An additional awareness event would be the promotion of a dependent care fair which would include community service providers, self-help groups, long term care insurance vendors, and workplace departments (such as the EAP) concerned with employee dependent care needs. This kind of a "benefits' fair" brings wide attention to the issue of concern, does not require a significant employee time commitment for participation, and brings community resources and caregivers together.

As was eluded to earlier, the utilization of a learn-at-lunch lecture series on dependent care is another method of bringing employee caregivers together in order to reduce any isolation they may be experiencing, while providing important information to assist them in the performance of their caregiving functions. Community agencies are usually appreciative of the opportunity to provide speakers and/or information, as part of their outreach mission. A variety of topics can be covered through such a format including legal, housing and financial needs, types of home-based and residential care, work schedule flexibility, altered family roles and communication patterns as well as education on medical/health-related topics.

Providing education to supervisors and managers on dependent care topics is also important. Supervisory/management training may include topics such as: (a) how to supervise employees who have flexible work schedules, (b) sensitization to the myriad demands upon those who are both caregivers and employees and (c) education on topics such as the human impact of coping with chronic illness, disability, as well as the processes of death/dying/grieving. Such training could be integrated into existing EAP supervisory training or it could be offered as a separate program.

The EAP can play an important role in advocating for and improving services for the dependent care population and their caregivers by engaging in collaborative organizing and program development activities with community dependent care providers. This would include supporting the development of elder care centers, respite care resources and other dependent care services by encouraging companies to make grants or contributions to community organizations that provide these services.

PREPARING THE EAP PROFESSIONAL
TO RESPOND TO THE NEEDS OF CAREGIVERS

The EAP practitioner responding to caregivers must have a thorough understanding of dependent care, including resources available in the community that address a variety of physical, emotional and practical needs. S/he must be prepared to assess dependent care as an underlying problem, even when an employee's statement of the presenting problem does not include caregiving responsibilities. Additionally, the EAP practitioner must be able to identify other problems associated with the caregiving role, including chemical dependency. She or he must be prepared to advocate for the client in obtaining legal, professional and practical services, and prepare the client for negotiating employment conditions necessary to carry on the dual role of caregiver and employee.

The EAP professional must understand a host of complex issues related to dependent care throughout the life cycle, including child development and child care, parenting, physical and mental health, disability, HIV+/AIDS, cancer and other life-threatening illnesses, the aging process, Alzheimer's disease and dementia, as well as death and dying. S/he must be knowledgeable about resources available, both within the organization and in the community. An EAP professional must also have a good understanding of the health care system, including health insurance and entitlements such as Medicaid, Medicare and SSI. S/he must understand the legal systems of conservatorship, guardianship and power of attorney, as well as mandated reporting of child and elder abuse.

Unfortunately, it may be that the majority of EAP providers do not currently possess an adequate knowledge and skill repertoire to be of optimal service to employees with dependent care needs. A survey of EAP counselors in New York found that less than one-quarter of respondents had ever attended a seminar or training program regarding elder care, let alone a more comprehensive program on dependent care (Brice and Gorey, 1989). EAPs must provide their counselors with comprehensive training that addresses these issues, and that offers practical skill-building opportunities in identifying dependent care as an issue related to a range of other presenting problems. Counselors must become well versed in providing comprehensive services that address the full range of issues associated with dependent care.

The need to be facile in dependent care assessment and referral capabilities is such that the EAP counselor cannot expect the client to identify dependent care as a presenting problem. The shift from spending time with a parent or partner to gradually assuming increased responsibilities can be subtle, as with the process of moving from social drinking to problem drinking to addiction. Dependent care is a problem with which the general populace has had limited experience and/or knowledge. However, it is a problem that will continue to grow, given the burgeoning aging population, as well as the proliferation of disabilities and diseases that threaten the very young to the very old. Employer assistance for employees experiencing the stresses of caring for a dependent (of any age) while continuing to hold a job will help the employer reduce costs, retain employees, and minimize the negative impact of the employee's dual responsibilities on her or his own work, as well as on the workplace as a whole.

THE FUTURE OF DEPENDENT CARE AND EAPs

More and more, the impact of dependent care needs on employees is receiving media attention through coverage within newspapers, tabloids and on network television. Topics addressed include the effect of employee dependent care needs on the workplace, as well as the adequacy of health care insurance and service delivery systems (including programs such as social security and medicare) in addressing dependent care needs. Until the health care insurance system provides adequate coverage and services for chronic illness and disability, caregiving will fall to individuals and families, the majority of whom are in the paid workforce.

For example, an adequate approach to benefit/service delivery structuring for dependent caregivers and those needing care is fully covered home attendant care, and a well trained and compensated pool of attendants to provide these services. Additionally, universal insurance coverage for long term institutionalized care, staffed with properly compensated and trained workers, would be of tremendous assistance to those who need it. Day programs outside the home, including adequate transportation and the ability to care for people with a variety of diagnoses, would also improve the lot of caregivers and their dependents. These services could be systematically coordinated and consistently delivered in communities throughout the United States.

Consequently, it is imperative that EAP professionals be advocating for the provision of dependent care benefits and programs, so as to minimize the impact of dependent care stressors on employees. EAPs have a responsibility to the employer and employees to try to address realities which can have an untoward and potentially negative impact on the capacity of employees to be optimally productive. Hopefully, the twenty-first century will see positive changes in making it easier, not harder, to provide and receive dependent care assistance. Until then, EAPs can play a vital role in giving voice to employee caregiver needs at the workplace.

REFERENCES

American Association of Retired Persons (AARP). 1987. A profile of older Americans: 1987. Washington, DC: American Association of Retired Persons.

American Association of Retired Persons (AARP) & The Travelers Foundation. 1988. *A National Study of Caregivers: Final Report.* Washington, DC: American Association of Retired Persons.

Brice, G.C., & K.M. Gorey. 1989. "EAP Coordinators Self-reported Competence to Handle Care Problems." Paper presented at the Annual Meeting of the Gerontological Society of America, Minneapolis, November.

Brody, E.M., P.T. Johnsen, M.C. Fulcomer, & A.M. Lang. 1983. "Women's Changing Roles and Help to Elderly Parents: Attitudes of Three Generations of Women. *Journal of Gerontology* 38: 597-607.

Brody, E.M., & C.B. Schoonover. 1986. Patterns of Parent Care When Adult Children Work and When They Do Not. *Gerontologist* 26: 372-381.

Chancellor's Advisory Committee on Dependent Care. 1994. *Elder/Adult Dependent Caregiving by U.C. Berkeley Faculty and Staff.* University of California, Berkeley.

Creedon, M.A. 1987. *Issues For An Aging America: Employees and Eldercare.* Bridgeport, CT: University of Bridgeport, Center for the Study of Aging.

Fortune Magazine and John Hancock Financial Services. 1989. *Corporate and Employee Response to Caring for the Elderly: A National Survey of U.S. Companies and the Workforce.* New York: *Fortune* Magazine.

Friedman, D.E. 1986. Eldercare: The Employee Benefit of the 1990's? *Across the Board* (June): 45-51.

George, L.K., & L.P. Gwyther. 1986. Caregiver Well-being: A Multidimensional Examination of Family Caregivers of Demented Adults. *Gerontologist* 26:253-60.

Green, G.P. & R.K. Epstein (Eds) 1988. *Employment and Earnings.* 35(2). Washington, D.C.: U.S. Department of Labor, Bureau of Labor Statistics.

Health Action Forum. 1989. *Employee Elder Caregiving Survey*. Boston: Health Action Forum of Greater Boston.

National Alliance for Caregiving & the American Association of Retired Persons (AARP). 1997. *Family Caregiving in the U.S.–Findings from a National Survey*. Bethesda, MD and Washington, DC: National Alliance for Caregiving and The American Association of Retired Persons.

Neal, M.B., N.J. Chapman, & B. Ingersoll-Dayton. 1987. Work and Elder Care: A Survey of Employees. Paper presented at the Annual Scientific Meeting of the Gerontological Society of America, Washington, DC, November.

Scharlach, A. 1988. *Survey of Caregiving Employees*. Los Angeles, CA: Transamerica Life Companies.

Scharlach, A., & S.A. Boyd. 1989. Caregiving and Employment: Results of an Employee Survey. *Gerontologist* 29: 382-87.

Scharlach, A., & K. Fredriksen 1992. *Survey of Caregiving Employees for the University of California, Berkeley*. Unpublished manuscript.

Scharlach, A., L. Midanik, C. Runkle, & K. Soghikian. 1992. Health Conditions and Service Utilization of Adults With Elder Care Responsibilities. Paper presented at the Annual Scientific Meeting of the Gerontological Society of America, Washington, D.C., November.

Sherman, R., A. Horowitz & S. Durmaskin. 1982. Role Overload or Role Management: The Relationship Between Work and Caregiving among Daughters of Aged Parents. Paper presented at the Annual Meeting of the Gerontological Society of America. Boston, November.

Soldo, B. & J. Myllyluoma. 1983. Caregivers Who Live with Dependent Elderly. *The Gerontologist*. 23: 607-611.

Stone, R.S., G.L. Cafferata, & J. Sangl. 1987. Caregivers of the Frail Elderly: A National Profile. *Gerontologist* 27: 616-626.

The Travelers Companies. 1985. *The Travelers Employee Caregiver Survey*. Hartford, CT: The Travelers.

United States Census Bureau, May 1995. *Sixty-Five Plus in the United States*. [http://www.census.gov/socdemo/www/agebrief.html]

United States Congress, Senate Special Committee on Aging, in conjunction with the American Association of Retired Persons, the Federal Council on the Aging, and the U.S. Administration on Aging. 1986. *Aging America: Trends and Projections, 1985-1986*. Washington, DC: U.S. Department of Health and Human Services.

Wagner, D., M. Neal, J. Gibeau, A. Scharlach, & J. Anastas. 1988. Eldercare and the Working Caregiver: An Analysis of Current Research. Unpublished manuscript. (Available from Donna Wagner, Center for the Study of Aging, University of Bridgeport, Bridgeport, CT 06601).

Walsh, W., R. Yoash-Gantz, M. Rinki, D. Loin, & D. Gallagher-Thompson. 1991. *The Use of Alcohol, Exercise, Smoking, and Psychotropic Drugs Among Female Caregivers*. Paper presented at the Annual Scientific Meeting of the Gerontological Society of America, San Francisco, California. November.

Employee Assistance and Work/Family Programs: Friends or Foes?

Patricia A. Herlihy

SUMMARY. The purpose of this chapter is to provide an overview of work/family programs and to indicate the similarities and differences between them and EAPs. Work/family initiatives can assist employees in garnering resources to manage the multiple and sometimes conflicting demands of work and family life. In addition to describing the history of work/family program evolution, information is also shared about the potential costs and benefits of an integrated model of service delivery between EAP and work/family programs. *[Article copies available for a fee from The Haworth Document Delivery Service: 1-800-342-9678. E-mail address: <getinfo@haworthpressinc.com> Website: <http://www.HaworthPress.com>]*

KEYWORDS. Work/family programs

INTRODUCTION

An interesting phenomena has evolved in the workplace over the last century. Companies have transitioned from a position which encouraged employees to keep all personal and family matters separate from their work, to today, where many companies have both an Employee Assistance Program (EAP) and a work/family program. These

[Haworth co-indexing entry note]: "Employee Assistance and Work/Family Programs: Friends or Foes?" Herlihy, Patricia A. Co-published simultaneously in *Employee Assistance Quarterly* (The Haworth Press, Inc.) Vol. 16, No. 1/2, 2000, pp. 33-52; and: *Emerging Trends for EAPs in the 21st Century* (ed: Nan Van Den Bergh) The Haworth Press, Inc., 2000, pp. 33-52. Single or multiple copies of this article are available for a fee from The Haworth Document Delivery Service [1-800-342-9678, 9:00 a.m. - 5:00 p.m. (EST). E-mail address: getinfo@haworthpressinc.com].

benefit service programs are company sponsored and address personal and family issues that can distract and interfere with an employee's ability to perform at work. A company's motivation for initiating and offering such programs, is that with today's fast paced, knowledge based, competitive marketplace, firms need workers who can fully concentrate on the task at hand and not be distracted by worries about childcare, health, financial or other personal problems.

Employee Assistance Programs and work/family programs have coexisted in some large companies for the last 10-15 years with little effort expended to examine the efficiency, effectiveness or functional differences between the two approaches. In an era of corporate re-design and overall analysis and redefinition of work functions, it is somewhat surprising that, no one has seriously examined or documented the differences and similarities, that exist between EAPs and work/family programs.

There is, however, considerable debate in the field as to where to draw the boundaries between these two programs. Some feel quite strongly that they should continue as completely separate programs, others are exploring synergies between the two and whether some type of integrated service might be appropriate. What has become recently clear through research (Herlihy, 1996), is that neither benefit program has accurate knowledge of what services the other program provides. This lack of awareness has resulted in territorial skirmishes and inefficiencies in the delivery of these two services.

The purpose of this chapter is to provide EAP practitioners with a current overview of the work/family arena. This information is offered for two reasons. First, EAP practitioners can benefit from the resources available to them in the work/family field; and second, it is important to stimulate policy discussions about the potential costs and benefits of an integrated model of service delivery between the two programs.

The manuscript is divided into the following sections:

   I. Definition of work/family programs
  II. The historical development of work/family programs
 III. The similarities and differences of EAP and work/family programs
  IV. Research on integration of EAPs and work/family programs
   V. The current issues in the field of work/family
  VI. The future for EAP and work/family programs

I. DEFINITION OF WORK/FAMILY PROGRAMS

An official definition of work/family is somewhat elusive. Whereas the EAP field has official definitions (EAPA, 1998; EASNA, 1991) and a suggested core technology (Roman, 1988); the work/family field has neither. The work/family field is at an earlier stage of development and only recently has initiated the goal of setting general standards and a certification process. For the purposes of this article the following general definition will be used to address what constitutes work/family programs:

> . . . organizational change strategies that involve a mix of policies and programs aimed at facilitating the integration of work and family roles. These include work/family and work/life programs and other initiatives aimed at integrating work and non-work demands. (Cutcher-Gershenfeld, 1997, p. 23)

To break this down further, work/family *policies* generally include areas such as: parental leave (Family Medical Leave Act), flextime, part time work, job sharing, flexible spending accounts, and dependent care accounts. *Work/family programs*, on the other hand, include a myriad of services for employees and their families which encompass the whole life span. For example, consultations, referrals and/or educational materials can be offered on topics ranging from: working during pregnancy, choosing a daycare facility, father support groups, summer camps, choosing a private school, college planning, managing money, caring for older relatives, and planning for retirement. Not every company provides all these services under the work/family umbrella. The extent of services is highly dependent on company size and the specific corporate culture. It is also important to note that various names are currently utilized to market these various services: life balance; work life effectiveness, and work/life initiatives in an attempt to reach a broader workforce population (Friedman, 1998).

According to the 1998 Survey of Work Life Initiatives (Friedman, 1998) there are 12 categories of work/family initiatives:

- flexible work arrangements
- time off policies
- child care initiatives
- elder care initiatives
- health care initiatives

- information and counseling support
- financial assistance
- training
- convenience services
- strategic alliances
- community investment
- implementation and evaluation

This list is clearly all inclusive and ambitious. Approximately 55% of the respondents from this particular survey (Friedman, 1998) related that they had no official name for these various initiatives and that they were housed in various departments throughout the company. Therefore, work/family or whatever title one prefers, seems to be an amorphous animal differing from the EAP field, which has more commonly identified services.

The more traditional work/family services such as child and elder resource and referral tend to follow casework models of identifying the issue, examining the parameters of the issue and deciding with the employee, the timing of when they need the information. Length of service can range from single session crisis intervention, to three or four months of ongoing services' receipt. The latter is most common for elder care cases. Despite variation in the nature of service delivery, follow up is an important piece of the overall service plan of most work/family programs.

In many larger companies there has been a shift to move beyond merely providing work/family policies and programs. The goal of this movement has been to develop "family friendly" cultures in the workplace. A family friendly or worker friendly culture translates into a work environment that supports and understands the outside interests and responsibilities of employees and thus, allows for flexibility and creativity in how work is done. Johnson and Johnson company is a wonderful early example of how to translate the notion of a family friendly environment into a business agenda. In 1989, the firm changed its company credo by adding the following statement: "We must be mindful of ways to help our employees fulfill their family responsibilities."

In order to fully appreciate the work/family field it is helpful to examine its historical roots, and to understand them in the context of their parallels with the EAP field. The next section will address the question of how the work/family field evolved.

II. THE HISTORICAL DEVELOPMENT
OF WORK/FAMILY PROGRAMS

The historical roots of the work/family movement actually date back to colonial times when the family was the most important social unit in society. During this period of history, work efforts that were required each day, were not separate from family functions. Gradually during the pre-industrial period, this changed. The place where work was performed became separate and distinct from the home. Men went off to counting houses, factories and mills and were paid for their work.

The emergence of any type of "work/family" program first appeared during the Civil War. Women were needed in the war effort, therefore, caretakers were needed for their children. Thus, the concept of an on-site child care center evolved. It is reported that it was a manufacturer of soldiers' clothing, who was the first to provide on-site child care (Friedman, 1991). "By 1910, the Association of Day Nurseries recorded the existence of 450 child care centers in working class neighborhoods. Some of these nurseries were actually sponsored by the factories where these mothers were employed" (Friedman, 1981 p. 22).

The next major development in the work/family field came around the turn of the century. Business leaders realized that wages, while necessary, were not sufficient to maintain their workforce. Workers needed to be housed and fed. They needed to be acculturated and properly trained and educated for the industrial society. Companies responded by establishing company restaurants and stores. The US Steel Company once owned more than 28,000 houses for their employees (Brandes, 1976). Schools were begun for employees and their children. By 1900, various American firms operated every form of school short of college. Toddlers could attend the company kindergarten, children the company grammar school, and even some company high schools were available (Brandes, 1976).

Taken together these practices comprise what has become known as "welfare capitalism." Brandes (1976) defines welfare capitalism as "any service provided for the comfort or improvement of employees which was neither a necessity of the industry nor required by law." Welfare capitalism was perceived by some, as businesses' attempt to co-opt the employee and his family into the belief that they were all one big happy family.

With the arrival of World War II came the transformation of the nation, its economy, the workplace and its people for the remainder of the 20th century. Although the 1930's saw some quibbling over the propriety of women taking jobs that rightfully belonged to men, the war ended this debate. The image of "Rosie the Riveter" captured the patriotic movement of women in the workplace. Almost half of all women held a job outside the home during the war (Sidel, 1986). While women worked, there was a need for child care. Nearly 3,000 child care centers were established at or near manufacturing plants during WW II under the Lanhan Act (Friedman, 1990). The two most famous of these centers were the two family-centered child care programs at the Kaiser Shipyards in Oregon and California. These centers were open 24 hours a day, 365 days per year and remained in existence for a period of 22 months (Morgan, 1967).

The 1950's have often been referred to as the "Golden Age." After the Great Depression and World War II, the idea of a family living in suburbia with a backyard barbecue and a house full of children was quite alluring (Mintz, 1988). Families turned from the public stresses and strains of the previous two decades inward to their own private lives. Individuals married earlier and had more children, and there was a renewed emphasis on family and togetherness.

In actuality, it was during the 1950's that an increasing separation between work and family evolved. With the mass movement of families out to the suburbs, frequently came a greater geographical distance from work. Commuting husbands, became night time residents or weekend guests in the eyes of the children. Since fathers were away from home, mothers ran the household. Yet, at the same time, corporate America did an excellent job socializing the family into corporate life. There were even books to inform corporate wives how they should respond in social situations (Whyte, 1956).

The dramatic rise in marriages that prevailed after World War II and into the 1950's was accompanied by an unprecedented baby boom. During the 1950's a million more children were born each year than during the 1930's (Mintz, 1988). The baby boom peaked in 1957 when the fertility rate stood at 3.7 children per woman. While this boom continued into the 1960's, by 1970 the fertility rate had fallen below the replacement level of 2.1 (Wetzel, 1990). The cohort of baby boomers affected many aspects of American life as they grew up, and continue to have significant impacts on today's labor markets (Dychtwald, 1997).

During the Great Society of the 1960s the federal government sponsored the formation of county-based "child care coordinating councils." These programs were designed to coordinate child care resources for pre-school children so that Head Start centers would be located to best reach the targeted children. The "4-Cs" as these councils came to be known were the foundation on which child care resource and referral services were created in the early 1980s (Burud, 1984). The "4-Cs" created a visibility for the shortages of care, which resulted as women entered the workforce at unprecedented levels during the 1960s and 1970s.

By the early 1980s, there was a significant increase in on-site day care centers, particularly in hospitals. In 1982 a national survey documented the existence of 152 hospital base child care centers and 42 industry based ones (Burud, 1984). However, it was the creation of employer sponsored child care resource and referral (R&R) services in the early 1980s, which is credited for the beginnings of the work/family and subsequently the work/life industry. Regional networks linking county-based R&Rs quickly became national networks. By 1985 there were several private companies administering R&R networks for large multisite employers (Phillips, 1997). By offering to assist employees in finding and managing their child care arrangements, employers validated this agenda and created a new function for their human resource departments. Once this agenda was validated as a business issue, employees were able to voice their needs and concerns more openly.

One very popular benefit that arose in the early 1980s was the Dependent Care Assistance Plans (DCAP). In 1981, the Economic Recovery Tax Act made dependent care a nontaxable benefit. As a result, employees could use pre-tax dollars for their child and elder care expenses. This particular benefit continues to be the most popular work/family benefit in most corporations today (84%).

Towards the end of the 1980s, the focus of the work/family field shifted. Many employer sponsored child care referral services had expanded to include issues regarding employees' elder parents and relatives. This was a controversial development, in that many EAPs had already been providing services in the elder care arena. Thus, the debate ensued over whether EAPs or work/family programs were better equipped to handle these employee needs.

Between the early and late 1980s the child care movement had evolved into the work/family movement. Another change was the move from merely providing assistance with dependent care issues, to the notion of finding a balance between work and family life. Some companies changed the names of these programs to work/life or work/life management in an attempt to broaden their appeal to all workers, whether single or married with children. This broadening of the target population, brought about a great deal of interest in flexible work schedules, job sharing, telecommuting and other creative working arrangements to cover other life needs of employees.

Elder care was another concern that emerged in the latter part of the 1980's. In 1986, 30 million Americans were over age 65, accounting for 12% of the population. Friedman (1990) cites that by the year 2030, senior citizens will account for 20% of the population. As a function of this burgeoning, work/family programs began developing resource and referral services for elder care. This was a controversial development as many EAPs had already been providing some form of services in the elder care arena. Thus, the debate ensued over whether EAPs or work/family programs were better equipped to handle these employee needs.

Child and elder dependent care as well as life balance interests have continued throughout the 1990's, despite widespread downsizing and worry that work/family issues might be set aside during economic hard times. Instead, the work/family field has grown from simply providing programs for employees and their families, to helping business understand the need for creating "effective" work environments. As mentioned earlier, currently there is a movement in the work/family field to facilitate a "family friendly culture" in the workplace.

This brief historical overview was presented to help EAP practitioners understand some of the influences that have shaped the work/family field. Now it is time to look at the specific similarities and differences of these two programs.

III. THE SIMILARITIES AND DIFFERENCES OF EAP AND WORK/FAMILY PROGRAMS

At the most abstract level EAP and work/family programs share a common goal of helping employees cope with personal issues in order to enable them to be productive and effective workers on the job. The differences between these two programs revolve around the specific services provided and the qualifications of the providers.

There continues to be lively debate in the field about which programs should provide which services. Clearly, the many variations depend on company culture and business priorities. Table 1 below is a general list of the similarities and differences of these two programs.

As one can see from Table 1, EAP and work/family programs provide many similar services. The real differences regarding services arise from the overall approach taken by the company's benefits staff to the employee's presenting concern. Historically, EAPs have had a more "problem" focus and dealt with issues from a clinical perspective. Work/family programs, on the other hand, have dealt with issues from a "solutions" focus and on a cognitive, educational level.

The large majority of EAP personnel are MSWs or PhDs and frequently certified as CEAP counselors. Only within the last year has the Alliance for Work Life Professionals (AWLP) initiated a potential certification process. Early in the life of the work/family field, many professionals had strong backgrounds in early childhood education. This no longer seems to be a major criteria for working in this field. Today many of the work/family professionals come from diverse business backgrounds rather than a clinical or educational one. Staff qualifications and capabilities are important issues to be explored when examining the possibilities of linkages of these two programs.

The following case example highlights the different foci these two professions bring to employees' concerns. This hypothetical case was called into an external EAP and then subsequently called into the external work/family vendor of the same parent company.

Case Example

Male employee calls the help line (an external vendor) asking for help obtaining child care for his 5 and 3 year old children. He has a major board meeting in the morning and needs coverage ASAP. His mother who has been taking care of his children, has recently refused to continue, due to his wife's returning home from having been discharged from a psychiatric hospital. The gentleman calmly mentions that his wife is currently passed out on the floor.

The EAP professional who answered this call conducted an excellent mental health assessment and dealt very effectively with the crisis of the wife's relapse. Calls were made to the psychiatric hospital that had discharged her, and a readmission was arranged for that evening. The work/family professional who received the exact same call lis-

TABLE 1. Similarities and Differences Between EAP and Work/Family Programs

Services Provided	EAP	Work/Family
Mental Health Counseling	Assessment and Referral of Mental Health Issues	Not officially provided by W/F Programs
Substance Abuse Counseling	Assessment, Referral and Follow Up of Substance Abuse Problem	Not provided by W/F Programs
Child Care Resource and Referral	Only a few EAPs provide this and usually from a National Data Base	Specialize in this area
Elder Care Resource and Referral	A few EAPs provide this service	Specialize in this area
Consultation on Life Events	yes	yes
Lunch time Seminars on topics such as parenting, stress management, etc.	yes	yes
Provide Educational Materials about key topics	Yes–mostly in the areas regarding mental health concerns	Yes–on almost any topic around personal issues for employees
Trauma Intervention	yes	no
Organizational Consultation	Yes–historically a part of EAPs	Yes–a new development in W/F
Policy Development	Yes, particularly regarding health care issues, i.e., AIDS, & Drug testing	Yes, particularly around scheduling issues, i.e., Parental leave, flextime, & telecommuting
Strategic Player in creating a "family friendly" work environment	Not currently a focus of EAP	Main thrust of many current work/family initiatives

tened carefully to the employees most urgent request for daycare. She found an appropriate child care arrangement for both children for the very next morning, in time for the employee's board meeting.

In this particular example neither the EAP nor work/family professional dealt with the whole situation. The EAP practitioner did not help the employee with the childcare concerns, and the work/family practitioner did not address the issue of the wife's psychiatric crisis. Unfortunately, this type of narrow focus in both programs currently exists in many companies across the country. For this very reason, some companies are exploring the possibility of a more integrated form of service delivery of these two programs.

Earlier it was mentioned that EAPs and work/family programs have co-existed in corporations for the last 10-15 years with little effort expended to examine their similarities and differences. The following section will briefly present a research project that attempted to explore the nature of these two programs, and any current linkages in service and policy.

IV. RESEARCH ON INTEGRATION OF EAPs AND WORK/FAMILY PROGRAMS

In 1994 Boston University's Center on Work and Family conducted the *National Survey of EAP and Work/Family programs*. The intent of the study was to explore the range of EAP and work/family service offerings as well as the interrelationship between these two programs. Specifically, this study focused on the relationship and linkages between EAP and work/family programs of companies with over 1,000 employees. The following is the basic demographic information from this research project.

Sample. A national study group consisting of 100 Corporations with employee populations of 1,000 or more were selected from established lists of family friendly companies. The work/family manager and EAP director of 127 companies were approached to participate in the survey in the hope of obtaining a final sample pool of 100 companies. A total of 96 companies responded from either the EAP or work/family programs, giving the study an overall response rate of 76 percent. A total of 78 companies responded from both the EAP and work/family departments within the company, providing a response rate of 61 percent. A total of 176 surveys were returned.

Corporate Profiles. Employee populations at the responding companies ranged from 1,233-313,000, with the average number of employees at 51,899. A cluster analysis of the geographical spread of responding companies is as follows:

Geography:

> Eastern Region–43%
> Midwestern Region–29%
> Southern Region–15%
> Western Region–13%

In terms of the type of industry respondent firms represented, Figure 1 indicates that the largest three industrial sectors represented: (a) financial/insurance companies, (b) manufacturing and (c) chemical companies.

EAP Profile and Characteristics. The EAP sample included a slightly higher proportion of internal EAPs (24%) than the frequently quoted number of 20% (Roman, 1990). Also, there was a fairly high number of companies with both an internal and external component to their EAP (35%). Only 42% of the study population had an external EAP service, compared to the 80% which is frequently quoted in the literature. The years in existence of EAPs ranged from two to thirty-eight years, with 10 years as the median.

Work/Family and EAP Comparisons. Since work/family programs are a comparatively recent benefit, differences in length of existence between these two programs, as reflected in Table 2 below, were not surprising.

One key finding of this research was that EAP and work/family programs viewed themselves as separate programs for the most part.

FIGURE 1. Industry

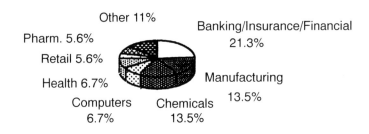

TABLE 2. Difference in Length of Work/Family and EAP Programs

Years in Existence	Work & Family	EAP
0-11 months	10.6%	0%
1-2 years	28.2	2.9
3-5 years	39.4	8.6
5 years plus	21.2	89.5

In order to understand this finding more clearly two descriptive results of the research will be presented. First, the question of extent of integration will be addressed, and then the respondents' rationales for separation of these programs will be examined.

Extent of Integration Between Work/Family and EAP. Survey respondents were asked the following questions about integration: (a) *Is there any interface/linkage between the EAP department and the work/family program in your company? and, (b) Are there any current plans to integrate the work/family and EAP programs in the company?* The results as summarized in Table 3 demonstrate that 76% of the EAP and 71% of the work/family respondents answered positively to the question about the existence of linkages between the two programs. However, when asked about whether they had any plans to integrate, only 28% of EAP and 26% of work/family answered in the affirmative. This result was surprising in that both programs seemed to understand a need to collaborate on some level, but were not interested in actually integrating their services. This finding was initially puzzling, until it was linked with the following survey question.

Rationale for EAP and Work/Family Practice Models. Survey respondents were asked: *If there is a separation between the EAP and work/family initiatives in your company, which of the following reasons most accurately describes the rationale for that policy?* As can be seen in Figure 2 below, the overwhelming response was that EAP and work/family programs were historically developed as separate entities (EAPs 81% and W/F 69%). Whereas EAPs were developed to keep "troubled" workers on the job, work/family programs evolved to help the new influx of working mothers stay on the job by addressing child care needs. There are both similarities and differences in how these two programs originated and evolved. The similarities revolve around key individuals articulating the need for either alcoholism or child care services. For EAPs the most notable individual was Dr. Daniel Lynch from New England Telephone. He initiated the first program for alcoholics in industry in the 1930s. Dr. Lynch and subsequent medical directors were strong advocates for rehabilitating alcoholics and returning them to the workplace as productive workers. For work/family, several distinct constituencies with sometimes competing agendas initiated and advocated the impetus for work/family reform in the 1960s (Pleck, 1991). Their initial focus was on increasing child care opportunities. Another similarity was that both programs challenged corporations to accept a workplace role in what had been generally perceived as an individual or "family" problem.

On the other hand, differences in how EAPs and work/family programs originated and evolved seem to have had an impact on program foci. As Figure 2 illustrates, different foci was the second most frequent response reported by 44% EAPs and 44% of W/F. In addition to the distinct initial foci of alcoholism and child care, both programs have continued along slightly different paths. As mentioned earlier, EAPs have remained more problem oriented and are staffed, for the most part, by clinicians. Work/family has taken a more solutions approach and tends to provide more cognitive and informational services.

The fact that these two programs were developed in different time periods (OAPs-1940s; W/F 1970s) and emerged with different foci, must be taken as only a partial explanation of the lack of integration. There was a discrepancy between the quantitative data and the qualitative data in this section of the research. Many respondents wrote comments or verbally communicated that the "real problem" with

TABLE 3. Integration Questions

Integration	No		Yes		Already Integrated	
	EAP	W/F	EAP	W/F	EAP	W/F
Linkages between EAP and W/F	24%	29%	76%	71%	–	–
Plans to integrate	72	74	16	11	12	15

FIGURE 2

Separation of EAP/WF

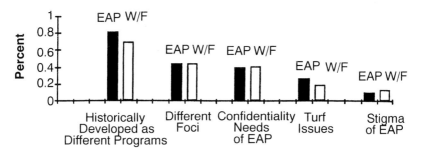

integration of these programs has to do with confidentiality of case information, although only 40% of respondents selected that reason. In particular, EAP professionals were more likely to see confidentiality as a barrier. This concern was highlighted by a *Wall Street Journal* article *"If You Use Firm's Counselors, Remember Your Secrets Could Be Used Against You"* (May 26, 1994) which reported that some companies were using information from the EAP to determine who was to be laid off. This article sent a chill through the backbone of the EAP community, particularly since a majority of firms were in the midst of major restructuring and downsizing efforts. As a researcher it is unclear whether one gives more "weight" or credence to qualitative or quantitative data. In this survey, many respondents deviated between the quantitative responses, where they needed to check the appropriate box, versus the qualitative responses which simply asked for their comments. Perhaps, because I am first a clinician, then a researcher, I tend to listen with slightly more vigor to the qualitative comments.

With that confession, the second most "talked about" reason for differentiating the EAP and work/family programs was that of social "stigma." Work/family respondents claimed that they did not want to be associated or "pulled down" by EAP stigma and preferred to address the "normal" adaptational coping issues of the everyday employee. Even though quantitatively the issue of stigma was ranked fifth at 10% and 14% in this survey, the "open ended" comments indicated that the issue of EAP stigma is deep rooted and one that creates a serious stumbling block to any integration of these two programs. One work/family manager commented that EAPs are generally "viewed as the last resort," whereas work/family is more "a first line of defense."

Turf issues were ranked fourth and reported by 27% of the work/family respondents and 19% of the EAP respondents. Although few respondents were comfortable talking about the specifics of these turf issues, many alluded to problems. With re-organization, downsizing and layoffs being front page news, everyone including EAP and work/family professionals are wondering about the security of their own jobs. Given the corporate climate, the thought of collaborating or perhaps "giving up" a piece of one's job, however perceived, may impact an individual's openness to the question of integrating services.

After reviewing the qualitative data regarding the question about integrating EAP and work/family programs, it became clearer that the key positive indicators for integration were: a corporate culture that supported and encouraged interdisciplinary efforts; and an internal champion who was invested in providing an integrated service to their employee population. This brief overview of the BU research project was provided to assist the reader in understanding the climate regarding collaboration between the EAP and work/family fields back in the mid 1990s. Time marches on and there are continual changes in the work/family field. The following section highlights current trends in the work/family field.

V. THE CURRENT ISSUES
IN THE FIELD OF WORK/FAMILY

The field of work/family has continued to forge ahead on many fronts. Three current themes of this forward movement are:

- Formation and sharp growth of the Alliance of Work Life Professionals
- Media blitz on the topic of work and family
- Strategic positioning of work/family as a major business player

In February, 1997 in San Diego, an inauguration meeting was held of the newly-merged national association for the Alliance of Work Life Professionals (AWLP). This combined the Association of Child Care

Consultants (ACCCI) from the mid 1980s and the National Work and Family Alliance from the early 1990s into one large umbrella organization. Over 325 consultants, corporate executives, academics, researchers, providers and labor leaders met to discuss the future of the work/family field. A topic of conversation that permeated this groundbreaking meeting was the need for partnerships. The range of partnerships discussed spanned managerial and worker teams, to collaborative efforts between government, corporations and communities. Relative to the EAP field, AWLP was encouraged to create strategic alliances with organizations such as EAPA. This creation of a national association for work/family professionals is a major milestone in the formal development of this field, and one that EAP professionals should watch.

The second issue revolves around the ongoing media blitz regarding the topic of work/family. In 1989 Felicia Schwartz wrote a controversial article in the *Harvard Business Review* which was later coined, the "Mommy Track." This article delineated two career tracks for women: namely, a professional career, or the "Mommy Track." Since the article's appearance, a major debate has occurred in the media over women's right to work and the consequences of this "supposed" choice. Numerous articles have appeared in academic journals, trade journals and popular magazines focusing on establishing a reasonable balance between work and family life. The *Wall Street Journal* initiated a weekly column devoted to a myriad of issues regarding work and family. For the last ten years *Working Mother* magazine has annually published a list of the top 100 best companies for working mothers. In September, 1996 *Business Week* began its own survey of the top family friendly companies. Nearly ten years after Schwartz's article, another controversial book has been published, *The Time Bind*, by Arlie Hochschild (1997), a researcher from University of California, Berkeley. The premise of this book arises from research conducted at a small midwestern company. Hochschild argues that people are escaping to work to avoid the messy problems of homelife. Some charge that this book is fueling a backlash against working women. Much like Schwartz, ten years earlier, Hochschild feels that her findings have been misunderstood. Regardless of the book's intent, it continues to fuel media attention around the priorities and balance people set between their work and family lives.The latest book in this arena, *Ask the Children* by Ellen Galinsky (1999) focuses its research on direct interviews with children of working parents and their reactions, feelings and thoughts about all of this.

The third theme chosen for discussion is the emergence of work/family professionals as no longer merely providers of corporate benefit programs, but legitimate players at the business table. Champions in this field have pushed to gain entrance to corporate decision making bodies in order to educate them about the role work/family can play in helping achieve crucial business goals. These professionals have encouraged decision makers to treat work/family as a legitimate management initiative comparable to quality management or process reengineering (Brown, 1997). A few companies, such as Eli Lilly, have begun to separate the work/family function into two components, strategic planning and service programs. Not everyone views these changes as positive. Some in the field are anxious about companies using this as a way to "downsize" the resources and staffing previously delegated to work/family programs and initiatives.

These three current themes in the work/family field were presented to help the EAP practitioner understand the constantly shifting sands of another field. Now let's turn to the question of the future of EAP and work/family.

VI. THE FUTURE FOR EAP
AND WORK/FAMILY PROGRAMS

The future of both EAP and work/family programs remains unclear. Mergers, corporate restructuring and work redesign have become a way of life in the business world. The increasing role of managed behavioral health care, and restructuring of human resource departments (Laabs, 1996), makes it highly unlikely that these programs will remain as currently conceived and delivered. Both the EAP and work/family fields need to continually assess and evaluate their relevance and contribution to the company's bottom line.

Clearly, employees in today's fast paced, stressful world of work, continue to need policies and services that support an appropriate balance between work and non-work demands. It is interesting to note that historically there seems to be a swing back to less separation between work and family as in colonial America. Work and family spheres are less separate today than they were back in the 1950's. Thus, what is needed is an acceptance of this shift and the building of a work culture that supports this change. The question remains, what is the most effective and efficient avenue to develop a culture which is supportive of employee needs while constantly keeping an eye on the bottom line.

EAP practitioners need to be open to new possibilities, whether this means partnering with work/family programs, wellness programs or managed care programs. Consolidation of effort seems to be the way of the future, as well as a more powerful tool in advocating for a more employee friendly workplace. For the last 50 years the EAP field has made crucial advances in the corporate world in terms of maintaining the productivity of the workforce. With the 21st century upon us, new opportunities and challenges arise. Employees and employers still very much need EAP services, but perhaps it is time to strengthen our mission by joining forces in creating a better overall work environment.

REFERENCES

Brandes, Stewart. (1976). *American welfare capitalism 1880-1940*. Chicago: University of Chicago Press.

Brown, Choral and Winter, Hope. (1997). The bottom line benefits of being a work/life leader. *Benefit Solutions*, March, 54-56.

Burud, Sandra, Aschbacher, Pamela, and Miecroskey, Jacquelyn. (1984). *Employer Supported Child Care: Investing in Human Resource*. Dover, MA: Auburn House.

Cutcher-Gershenfeld, Joel; Kossek, Ellen and Sandling, Heidi. (1997). Managing concurrent change initiatives: Integrating quality and work/family strategies. *Organizational Dynamics*. Winter. 21-36.

Dychtwald, Ken. (1997). How changing demographics have affected work/life field–The baby boomer generation issues. Presentation at the Alliance Conference, San Diego, CA.

Friedman, Dana. (1998). *Survey of Work/Life Initiatives*. William Mercer/Bright Horizons.

Friedman, Dana. (1991). Linking work-family issues to the bottom line. N.Y.: The Conference Board.

Friedman, Dana. (1981). Management by parent objectives. Dissertation, Harvard University, Cambridge, MA.

Galinsky, Ellen. (1999). *Ask the Children*. Fairfield, N.J.: W. Morrow Co.

Herlihy, Patricia. (1996). Examination of integration of EAP and Work/Family programs. Dissertation, Florence Heller School, Brandeis University, Waltham, MA.

Hochschild, Arlie. (1997). *The time bind: When work becomes home and home becomes work*. New York: Metropolitan Books.

Ingram, David. (1998). America @ Work: An overview of employee commitment in America. AON Consulting Firm.

Laabs, Jennifer. (1996). Downshifter: Workers are scaling back–Are you ready?. *Personnel Journal*. March, 62-76.

Mintz, S. and Kellogg, S. (1988). *Domestic revolution: A social history of the American family life*. N.Y.: The Free Press.

Pleck, Joseph. (1991). Work-Family policies in the United States. In Hilda Kahn and Janet Giele's *Women's Lives and Women's Work: Parallels and Contrasts in Modernizing and Industrial Countries*. Boulder, CO: Westview Press.

Roman, Paul and Blum, Terry. (1988). The core technology of employee assistance programs: A reaffirmation. *The Almacan*. 18(8), 17-22.

Schultz, Ellen. (1994). If you use firm's counselors, remember your secrets could be used against you. *Wall Street Journal*. 5/16, C1-C6.

Schwartz, Felicia. (1989). Management women and the new facts of life. *Harvard Business Review*. January-February, 65-76.

Stevenson, Rachel. (1942). Absenteeism in an industrial plant due to alcoholism. *Quarterly Journal of Studies on Alcohol*. 2:661-668.

Trice, H. and Schonbrunn, W. (1981). A History of job-based alcoholism programs: 1900-1955. *Journal of Drug Issues*. Spring, 171-198.

Wetzel, J. (1990). Family related benefits in the workplace. *Monthly Labor Review*. March, 28-33.

Whyte, William. (1956). *The Organization Man*. N.Y.: Simon and Schuster.

EAP Services to Older Adults
in the Workplace:
A Strengths Perspective

Kathleen Perkins

SUMMARY. The focus of this article is to address the burgeoning number of older employees in the workforce, and their needs regarding services and pre-retirement planning. By using a strengths-based model, prevention-focused interventions are suggested which an EAP could assist in facilitating at the workplace, thereby enhancing employee retirement options. *[Article copies available for a fee from The Haworth Document Delivery Service: 1-800-342-9678. E-mail address: <getinfo@haworthpressinc. com> Website: <http://www.HaworthPress.com>]*

KEYWORDS. Older employees, strengths-based services, retirement planning

As the number of older adults facing retirement in the population increases, the need to recognize their unique talents and skills also increases. As people live longer lives, many will spend as much time in retirement as they do in the workplace. In this chapter, work and retirement will be discussed in the context of EAP services to older adults from an indirect, macro perspective. The workplace will be used as metaphor for community; thus, via EAP services, the workplace is viewed as the hub for resources to aid in strengths' develop-

[Haworth co-indexing entry note]: "EAP Services to Older Adults in the Workplace: A Strengths Perspective." Perkins, Kathleen. Co-published simultaneously in *Employee Assistance Quarterly* (The Haworth Press, Inc.) Vol. 16, No. 1/2, 2000, pp. 53-75; and: *Emerging Trends for EAPs in the 21st Century* (ed: Nan Van Den Bergh) The Haworth Press, Inc., 2000, pp. 53-75. Single or multiple copies of this article are available for a fee from The Haworth Document Delivery Service [1-800-342-9678, 9:00 a.m. - 5:00 p.m. (EST). E-mail address: getinfo@haworthpressinc.com].

ment. The end sought is satisfied workers and/or comfortable retirement. The strengths perspective will be used to examine the concepts of work, retirement, and community resources. Work and retirement will be seen as a process rather than as singular events with the goal of promoting sound mental health throughout.

The method used to demonstrate how to augment older workers' strengths through EAP intervention will be that of prevention. Prevention is seen here as a tool for reducing stress, anxiety and depression, and enhancing the mental health of older adults in the workplace. Using a strengths perspective, there are a number of areas that EAP can assist by helping older adults make the necessary adjustments as they move back and forth between work and retirement. Some examples of EAP assistance are: (a) advocating for human resource policies which make retirement flexible and optional; (b) accessing models and/or creating models that offer innovative alternatives to retirement, such as job retraining and drawing on public and community resources to accommodate working needs of older adults; (c) pre-retirement planning to include income adjustment for retirement; and, learning how to use leisure time. A case example using the strengths perspective will be provided to demonstrate the various interventions EAP can use.

POPULATION GROWTH AND WORK STATUS

The growth rate of the elder population has been on an upward spiral for five decades. People over 65 in 1900 made up approximately 4 percent of the population in the United States. In 1990 12.6 percent of the population was 65 or older with 67.3 men for every 100 women (U.S. Bureau of the Census, 1991). This spiraling growth has evened off and we will see a slight decrease until 2010 when the baby boom generation starts to reach old age.

Older workers comprise less than 3 percent of the total labor force: 17 percent are men, 8 percent are women. Older workers are less likely to be in jobs that are physically demanding, low or entry level, or high-tech as compared to their younger counterparts. The trend toward early retirement has increased and part-time work for older people has expanded to over 50 percent of retired workers, especially among women (Hooyman & Kiyak, 1993). Part time-work status is often seen as desirable because the older person has the ability to draw partial pensions (AARP, 1991; Hooyman & Kiyak, 1993).

Even though part-time work is desirable, numerous obstacles exist. For example, such work may not be available at the same level of wages full-time employment is offered; usually there is a minimum number of hours required. Some employers have policies prohibiting part-time workers from drawing partial pensions and also Social Security places limits on the amount that can be earned at a given age before full benefits are reduced (Hooyman & Kiyak, 1993). There is good news, however, with Social Security restrictions. President Clinton signed into law The Senior Citizen's Right to Work Act which increases the amount older adults can earn from outside employment without jeopardizing their Social Security benefits. The increases will be phased in over seven years. Under the old law, those over 65 who continued to work were limited to earning $11,520 in outside income. Income over that could reduce their Social Security payments. In 1996 that jumped to $12,500, and it rises to $30,000 by 2002 (Welsh, 1996).

There are other barriers facing older workers seeking employment, most notably ageism, sexism and racism. Despite antidiscrimination legislation, there is still widespread age-based discrimination. Some of this discrimination toward older workers could exist because of negative stereotyping that endures despite research findings to the contrary. They include assumptions that older workers will not perform as well as younger workers because of poor health, declining energy, or diminished intellectual ability (Hooyman & Kiyak, 1993). What we know as fact is that the average number of absences among older workers is low as is the number of accidents, and often they are better job performers and more loyal to an organization than their younger counterparts (Kart, 1994). Other structural barriers are: skill obsolescence and age bias in the allocation of jobs, and lack of technical training.

To be discussed in more detail later in this chapter is how gender, race, and class figure into the equation of older persons in the workplace. The chapter focus is primarily on workers already in the workplace, but will also address the older worker who wishes to re-enter.

SOCIOECONOMIC PROFILE OF OLDER ADULTS

The three most compelling factors facing older adults today are income security, health and the provision of health care. Inextricably linked to these factors are work and retirement. Any discussion of retirement must be placed in the broader context of lifelong work experience.

Work force participation is an economic predictor for retirement. This prediction is especially significant for working-class men and women who have experienced labor market inequities (Perkins, 1993a). For women, evidence of this inequity is found in the fact that 77 percent of all employed females are working in low pay occupations and industries (National Commission on Working Women, 1986). This trend is expected to extend into the next century. The trend, however, will be somewhat different for the nation's baby boomers as they move toward retirement age. (See Tice & Perkins, 1996.) Nonetheless, this currently leaves scores of older women retiring into poverty (Perkins, 1993b). Women are especially hard hit, not only because they outlive men, but also because they often outlive their assets. (See Perkins, 1994.)

When women are examined within the broader context of lifelong work patterns, a clearer picture of their economic status emerges. Women frequently have interrupted work histories, specifically for reasons of caring for family members, and hold either part-time and/or low-paying, low status jobs (Perkins, 1993b). The poorest category amongst all the older adult groups is African American women (Gould, 1989).

Social Security and pension systems will have practically ended poverty among older men and couples by the year 2020. Poverty will remain widespread, however, among older women living alone; divorced, widowed or never married (Older Women's League, 1990). Poverty income guidelines in 1992 revealed that for a family of one, income less than or equal to $6,729, and for two, less than or equal to $8,487 signified an existence at or below poverty existence (Bureau of the Census, 1992).

The Social Security Act, drafted more than 50 years ago, best protects a family consisting of a lifetime paid worker, typically a husband, a lifelong unpaid homemaker, typically a wife, and dependent children. Seventy percent of older, nonmarried women, however, depend on Social Security as their sole income. This system is obviously outdated, and if left as it stands, future generations of women will continue to receive Social Security benefits that are significantly inadequate (Older Women's League, 1990).

Almost twice as many men than women over age 65 receive private pension income related to their own work record (46% vs. 23.5%) (Perkins, 1994). In 1991, the average yearly pension benefit for men over 65 was $7,059 compared to $3,647 for women (Leonard, 1994). African American older women, in general, receive lower Social Security benefits than white older women and are only half as likely as their white counterparts to receive a private pension (Gould, 1989; Perkins 1993a). The total monthly Social Security benefit for African American women age 65 to 69 in 1992 averaged $467. For white women, it was $512 (Social Security Administration, 1993).

A close second to income security in old age is health care concerns. Affordable health care is a problem when people are unemployed, ineligible for Medicare and Medicaid, and in the case of many women, employed in jobs without health care benefits. Most married women, in or out of the labor force, have private health insurance, but 40% of divorced women and 27% of widows who are not employed have no such benefits (Perkins, 1992). This means that four to five million older women spend much of their social security payments for health care (Stone, 1986).

Even those older adults who benefit from Medicare cannot rest easy. Within the current political climate, health care is in a state of flux. While the prospects for expanding coverage under Medicare seemed plausible early in 1994, the discussion in 1995 shifted to how much can be wrung out of the Medicare program to help balance the federal budget. Even if Medicare were separated from the budget discussion there will be a strain placed on public spending because of future demographics. It seems inevitable that the program will need to be streamlined (Moon, 1995).

THE WORKPLACE

The work lives of men and women are increasingly similar. Both seek feelings of competence, of making a contribution, of being necessary and productive, and of being in control of time and energy. The differences, however, are significant with regard to earnings and occupations (Perkins, 1992). Women and men are the same in that earnings are crucial to personal support and to support families (Report on Status of Midlife and Older Women, 1986). Women and men are not the same, however, in the amount of earnings they receive.

Women's salaries are not commensurate with those of men. Rather, women's earnings are substantially less (Report on Status of Midlife and Older Women, 1986). Women have earned an average of $0.64 for every $1.00 earned by men consistently since 1950 (Smith & Ward, 1984; Faludi, 1991). This gap has closed slightly (about 10%) in the past decade, not due to salary increases for women, but due to the decline in mens' salaries (Cory, 1993). Not only are there economic differences related to gender in the work force, there are differences related to race. African American women have a narrower sex-wage differential than white women due to the interaction of race and sex discrimination in hiring and promotion (Madden, 1985). Bergmann (1971) suggests that race discrimination can cause wage differentials among equally skilled occupations, and that wage differentials by race may be maintained through occupational segregation rather than overt wage discrimination.

An examination of differences in work histories among African American and white, male and female adult workers found African American women's work histories to be less continuous than those of African American and white males. African American women's work histories were less continuous than men's but more continuous than white women (Gibson, 1983). When the issues of impoverishment are examined solely with reference to gender, however, the plight of the black man is ignored or understated. It is true that women have a higher incidence of poverty than men of the same race; however, this generalization does not hold across races (Burnham, 1985; Sparr, 1986). For example, poverty rates for African American men are nearly double that for white women. Furthermore, for those African American women who continue to hold jobs, being employed full-time, on a year-round basis is no guarantee against poverty (Higgenbotham, 1986).

With these wage differentials, which have major implications for retirement income, drawing on strengths and the use of preventive techniques becomes an important advocacy intervention approach for EAP workers to help insure economic security in people's later life. These will be addressed in the latter section of this chapter.

CHALLENGES FOR THE OLDER WORKER

The older worker is defined as 50 to 80 years old. With the 1986 legislation eliminating mandatory retirement for most occupations, some older people choose to remain in the workplace. Some return to work after they have retired. In either event, most older workers face challenges in the work environment. Some of those challenges include retirement, coping with involuntary retirement, maintaining competitiveness in an increasingly technologically-based workplace and eldercare responsibilities.

Retirement

People retire for a variety of reasons, and they reenter the labor force for a variety of reasons. Retirement can be voluntary, based on the attainment of economic and psychological goals and/or based on a mutual agreement with a spouse; or it may be forced, because of extended periods of unemployment (e.g., discouraged worker), lack of employment opportunities, downsizing, gender and race discrimination, family responsibilities, or health problems. The decision to return to work is usually based on economic need, however, some people are not psychologically suited to retirement and choose to return to work for that reason.

Retirement involves three major periods–pre-retirement, transition, and post-retirement. The pre-retirement period typically involves looking ahead to a future life. It is a period during which decisions about whether and when to retire are made (Atchley, 1982). If economic security in retirement is to be realized, it is during the pre-retirement period that planning must occur (Hayes & Deren, 1990).

Pre-retirement planning (PRP) is probably the single most formidable means of prevention against post-retirement hardship known to many older adults. It can help to insure economic, social, and psychological well-being in late life. Unfortunately, PRP is a concept that has not been vastly utilized by older Americans over the last two decades. The greatest barrier to people obtaining PRP is availability. Retirement planning programs typically have not existed in most firms and companies until very recently (Perkins, 1994). Where PRP programs do exist, encouraging older workers to take advantage of them has been met with limited success. This is most likely due to the fears associated with retirement, that is, loss of status, growing old, impending death, and so forth (Perkins, 1994).

Much has been written on life satisfaction and quality of life in post-retirement. Both depend on the individual's personality, income, health, social circumstance, and sense of worth. Probably health and income are the more predominant predictors of quality of life, with the working-class being the most adversely effected by these two factors.

Early/Involuntary Retirement, the Role of EAP

There are a number of factors at work in the trend toward early retirement. The early retirement option under Social Security and the liberalizations in Social Security benefits have played a role along with the availability of private pensions. Situations differ considerable, however, depending on a person's health and retirement income status. Although early retirement has been widespread, especially for those financially able, there are serious concerns for many older people who find themselves unemployed (Morris & Caro, 1995).

There are vast numbers of older adults who find themselves involuntarily unemployed for reasons of ill health or structural unemployment in different geographic settings and, most recently, as the result of the brutal "downsizing" of corporate America, often accomplished through layoffs rather than early retirement incentives. Many unemployed older adults are willing and able to work: however, they have greater difficulty finding replacement jobs than younger workers and many have more difficulty changing fields (Morris & Caro, 1995). Because of these factors, new opportunities are needed for work force participation and employee assistance programs could be an innovative player in advocating for the provision of human resource policies which could provide those opportunities. Some initiatives might include developing or collaborating with regional and national EAP practitioners, state and local employment offices and organizations for human resource professionals to generate tailored analyses of local labor markets, career counseling, retraining, and placement services (Morris & Caro, 1995). These initiatives, along with other considerations for helping displaced older workers find their niches and maintain competitiveness, will be discussed under prevention and intervention. They all serve as examples of potential community building activities which can augment and enhance older workers' strengths.

The Caregiving Crisis

A more recent consideration for older workers and retirees is eldercare. The role of primary caregiver has a significant impact on women and their participation in the labor force. Approximately 2.2 million people provide unpaid care to frail elders at home. Of those, 72% are women and over half are 45 years and older, with an average age of 57 (Perkins, 1993b). More men are assuming greater caregiving roles than ever before, but the unpaid caregivers are overwhelmingly female. While women originally assumed the caregiving role because they were at home, their influx into the workplace has not significantly diminished their caregiving role; they simply do both (Perkins, 1993b). More than 8% of these women caregivers quit work; of those who continue to work, more than 20% reduce hours or take time off without pay (Stone et al., 1986).

What the above discussion implies, is that retirement needs to be flexible and optional. For those who need to work, the work must be dignified and healthy as well as providing flexible hours (Perkins, 1992). Many employers have begun to put innovative alternatives into practice, providing excellent models which others can follow. EAPs have the opportunity to promote the already existing models and/or create some of their own. One such creation would be the model outlined in this chapter using the workplace as a "community" full of resources for older workers to mine.

THE STRENGTHS PERSPECTIVE

The strengths perspective provides a useful framework for prevention and intervention services for older workers for several reasons. The model focuses on human potential, highlights positive client attributes, and facilitates collaborative client-worker relationships. This shift in orientation, away from emphasizing pathology and problems, is significant to EAPs because it: (1) carries the expectations for positive change and outcomes; (2) emphasizes assessment and service delivery involving a mutual enterprise between clients, their support systems and EAP workers; and, (3) presents an empowerment approach that encourages older workers to recognize and capitalize on their competencies in the face of personal challenges.

This does not mean that the problem definition is overlooked but rather that client strengths guide the intervention. Consequently, the method of assessing and building on strengths is flexible in its application and is intended for use with other approaches that EAP workers might use. Those approaches could involve a variety of direct services including clinical interventions.

KEY CONCEPTS

As seen in Figure 1, the key concepts of the strengths perspective are: *empowerment, suspension of disbelief, dialogue and collaboration, membership, synergy* and *regeneration*. The linchpin in the new practice model is the concept of *empowerment*: which means the EAP practitioner must seek out diverse settings where people are using their strengths to handle problems, and underscore to clients their competencies. As a result, clients are enlisted in gaining control over their lives (Rappaport, 1981).

A close corollary to the concept of empowerment is *suspension of*

FIGURE 1. Concepts of the Strengths Perspective: Foundations for a Strengths Model of Practice

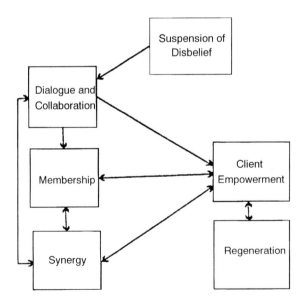

Source: Tice, C. & Perkins, K. (1996). *Mental Health Issues & Aging: Building on the Strengths of Older Persons*. Pacific Grove, CA: Brooks/Cole Publishing Company

disbelief, defined as acceptance of the client's "interpretive slant" of given situations (Saleebey, 1992). This counters any tendency to see clients as distorting the "truth" or reality.

Moving toward suspension of disbelief positively influences the strengths perspective's concept of *dialogue and collaboration* between clients and EAP practitioners as they work toward common goals. In a collaborative relationship, the EAP professional and the client seek to discover the individual and communal resources that will best facilitate the achievement of the client's wants or goals (Weick, Rapp, Sullivan, & Kishardt, 1989).

From collaboration and dialogue grows a sense of *membership* in family, friendship, and community networks. People without membership are extremely vulnerable due to their lack of supportive networks within communities of interest and care.

The strengths perspective contends that the coming together of person and community constitutes *synergy*: creating new energy and resources. *Regeneration*, the final concept of the strengths perspective, recognizes the capacity for change. This perspective is a radical departure from a problem or pathological orientation because instead of looking for external forces to solve a dilemma, social workers look to the innate abilities of clients (Weick, 1983).

WORKPLACE PREVENTION INTERVENTIONS: STRENGTHS-BASED FOR OLDER WORKERS

Prevention/Intervention

What is prevention and what can be expected from it? Prevention techniques include education, anticipatory guidance, disease prevention, and policy development (Rappaport, 1961). In the strict sense of the word, prevention means to keep a thing from happening. Loosely defined, for the purpose of this chapter, it will be considered more as an intervention. Rather than a long-term, pre-planned prevention, it will be used in the context of short-term prevention/intervention on a daily, weekly, monthly and yearly basis. Prevention/intervention will be addressed not only as it relates to individuals but also at the workplace/community level. The overall focus will be on strengths and empowerment, with the end result being lower stress, and anxiety, good mental health and enhanced productivity. Prevention activities for older workers could include offering workshops and lunchtime lectures on topics that address aspects of retirement planning such as: financial preparedness, use of leisure time, health maintenance and wellness activities, education on senior community resources, and information on obtaining post-retirement volunteer experiences or employment. Additional prevention interventions EAPs could engage in for older workers could include: (a) facilitating a needs assessment related to older worker dependent caretaking needs, (b) facilitating mutual aid/peer support groups, and (c) serving as an advocate or broker for older workers seeking EAP services associated with experiencing possible age-based discrimination. Another EAP prevention intervention would be to collaborate with human resources staff to provide assistance for older workers in outplacement and job retraining, particularly related to those losing jobs based on downsizing.

An example of a prevention intervention combining aspects of direct and indirect services is a time-limited mutual aid/peer support group for pre-retirees, facilitated by an EAP practitioner. Membership in the group would be open to anyone planning to retire; referrals could be made through benefits officers who provided retirement information to employees. The group could also be marketed through organizational communiques or broadcast through e-mail. Potential members would be screened by the EAP practitioner before the group began. A maximum of 12 people would be appropriate so as to facilitate communication and relationship building amongst members.

As a closed, time-limited mutual aid experience, eight to ten sessions would be appropriate. At each session there would be some specific content imparted to group members by the EAP professional; or, a community resource person. Group members would then discuss their reactions and intended actions pursuant to the content imparted. For example, a group session might focus on designing a "post-retirement" job description.

The prevention and community building aspects of this kind of facilitated mutual aid experience are numerous. First, participants acquire concrete information for use in retirement planning. Second, members develop mutual aid camaraderie of "all in the same boat." Third, members can maintain contact with each other, and extend the life of their mutual aid community experience as the time-limited group ends. In the context of the strengths model, it is a perfect opportunity for self-empowerment for all who participate. This automatically leads to a sense of membership and regeneration.

Within the next section, an elaboration of components of key prevention activities for older workers will be provided.

Pre-Retirement Planning

As noted previously, engagement in pre-retirement planning is critical in order to maximize the use of one's multiple strengths for retirement. Employee assistance programs can be on the cutting edge of advocacy for older workers not only by recognizing the need for pre-retirement planning, but by organizing, collaborating, and facilitating opportunities for older workers to take part in such planning. In the broad context, this type of intervention is viewed as a preventive approach promoting sound mental health. As has been well documented in the employee assistance field, employee well being is associated with employee productivity. Older workers are likely to feel an enhanced sense of being valued by employers if workplace-based retirement planning options are provided. Consequently, older worker's strengths can be augmented through programs/policies which send the message, "we care about you."

With so many companies experiencing restructuring, belief in lifetime employment stability that typically leads to retirement security can no longer be counted on. One of the most critical aspects of this change, for EAP consideration, is that of encouraging greater employee responsibility in preparing for retirement security. Many employees may have neither the skills nor interest in financial planning that are required to develop or execute a regular program of savings. Consequently, EAPs will need to sponsor education programs for employees stressing the need to save early, plan ahead for retirement, and provide opportunities for acquiring information on how to evaluate their options.

The changes of the 1990s will have an effect on the future of age-based policies. Some of these changes are reflected in organizational structure, compensation and benefits. As these issues play out, they are bound to have an impact on policy toward older workers. Employers are reexamining retirement strategies. Using the predictions for change by Rappaport (1995, p. 67), EAPs can assist older workers by allowing for the following topics to be covered in lunchtime lectures, workshops and similar prevention activities aimed at older employees:

1. An increasing need for employees to bear more responsibility for retirement and financial planning.
2. A reduction in employer coverage for Medicare-eligible retirees, and an increase in employee health care benefit contributions for retiree health at any age.
3. Increased focus on Medicare risk contracts as a way to cover retiree health.
4. A decline in employer support for benefits provided to all, and a shift in emphasis to matched savings programs.
5. A redesign of many pension plans to a cash balance or other approach that modifies the benefit accrual pattern while retaining the employer investment risk and favorable returns that can accrue from risk assumption.
6. Increased choice in investment options within employee savings and more savings education.
7. Continued focus on early retirement windows in special situations, and reductions in subsidies in non-window situations.
8. More options for gradual retirement.
9. Gradual increase in full retirement ages.
10. Continued use of corporate restructuring and accompanying elimination of jobs.
11. Increased focus on second and third careers.

Post-Retirement Return to Work as Prevention/Intervention

Another workplace prevention intervention is to actually encourage employees facing retirement to consider returning to work, post-retirement. Some older people return to work after retirement out of economic necessity. Others seek personal satisfaction out of paid employment. Whatever the reason, paid work can be seen as prevention/intervention for older adults in the form of added financial security and as an aid in warding off poor mental health. Perkins (1994, p. 90) lists some innovative work options for older people wanting employment:

1. Banks. With a life-time of managing their money, older workers excel as tellers and customer-service representatives. The Bank

of America in Los Angeles provides two weeks of training and typically pays $7 to $10 an hour.

2. Hotels. In 1985, two Days Inn found that the average employee quit after three months; this was accompanied by an absentee rate of 30%. Days Inn tapped the over-55 labor market and, today, in nearly a third of the centers, 450 employees are 55 or older. Their average tenure is three years; the absentee rate is 3%; the average salary is $6.50 an hour.

3. Hardware stores. Picture yourself roaming a hardware store in search of the right widget to fix the toilet. A mature face suggests years of fix-up experience to you. This is a lesson learned by home-improvement chains like Builders Emporium, where 15% of the 6,200 employees are over age 55, as well as Hechinger and Home Depot. A typical salary in a California Builders Emporium is $7.35 per hour.

Most older people require some retraining in order to step into the dignified and healthy jobs that will help sustain them financially. Few programs specifically provide retraining for older adults. An exception is the program Senior Community Services Employment (SCSE), which is funded by the Older Americans Act of 1965. This program provides part-time subsidized employment opportunities for older adults, making a difference both in their income and quality of life (Mor-Barak & Tynan, 1993; Perkins, 1994).

There are other programs that draw on public and community resources, and, to some extent, private industry. These programs for older workers typically fall into two categories. One facilitates linkages between older adults and potential employers. The other accommodates the needs of older adults in the workplace through job modification, job training, and senior care. For a full description of these programs see Mor-Barak and Tynan [1993] (Perkins, 1994).

Case Example: Using the Strengths of Older and Retired Workers to Empower Peers at the Workplace Through Pre-Retirement Planning

When looking for ways to approach prevention activities, e.g., pre-retirement planning for older workers, EAP staff can draw on Maslow's method of studying the "well-adjusted" rather than the "maladjusted." An example of use of the strengths perspective is an EAP staff who searched through past records and identified a number of older adults who were leading meaningful and zestful lives. Some had retired while others had reentered the labor market. The EAP staff contacted those former clients and secured their permission to participate in focus groups which would discuss how they were managing their lives. Space was provided by the EAP and transportation was offered to facilitate participation. Focus groups findings were then used in order to formulate a pre-retirement planning workshop program designed to help older employed workers who were having difficulty with the various transitions facing them in leaving and re-entering the workplace. Through the program workshops, the EAP staff worked with older adults to set new goals for themselves and to provide the support necessary for them to achieve their goals. Dialogue and collaboration undergirded the entire process, with an end result being the achievement of older employees' goals, by using the strengths of self-empowered older workers who were former EAP clients.

About one eighth (9) of the focus group members participated in the planning and implementation of the first workshop. Also included in the planning were five older employees representing their age peers in the workplace. This planning group also helped design questionnaires to survey all employees as to their perceived needs regarding retirement. The consensus was to focus on all employees 50 years of age and above. Survey results noted the following as needs of older workers:

1. flexible retirement policies

    - extended work life
    - rotating work schedules, i.e., work 3 (or 6) months; off 3 months
    - part-time job opportunities both temporary and permanent

2. adult day care for senior parents or spouses
3. job retraining
4. a bi-monthly newsletter
5. ongoing support and mutual aid groups addressing peer counseling, volunteering, computer technology, and post-retirement leisure time
6. fitness and wellness activities

As an example of empowerment and regeneration dynamics, one of the more prominent issues to emerge from the workshop was the need for older adults to move beyond the "work ethic" values of the middle years. It was determined that new "yardsticks" were needed for measuring what makes life worth living. While perseverance, industriousness, competence, and achievement are splendid values, they are not enough. To allow for holistic self-actualization, the proposed pinnacle of human development in Maslow's hierarchy of needs, further development is warranted to clarify its diverse attributes. For example, the cultivation of aliveness, playfulness, effortlessness, goodness, and meaningfulness seem especially appropriate qualities to value during the senior years. The freedom and leisure of senior years could provide the conditions for a more empowering self-actualization to occur than might be possible if notions of optimal human development focused only on factors of productivity and usefulness.

Out of the first PRP workshop grew the model to be used for future prevention interventions for older workers. As the last exercise in the workshop, sub-groups were formed as the nucleus for planning future PRP activities. Again, the strengths perspective components of empowerment, dialogue and collaboration, membership, synergy, and regeneration were used to do this. The EAP organizers designed this component of the program to serve as a prototype for future PRP activities. The goal was to include older adults in future training; consequently, the EAP organizers wanted to provide opportunities for member decision-making, management and control of operations through peer support. This approach taps participants' strengths that can lead to empowerment as well as promoting dynamics of membership, synergy and regeneration.

Having provided an example of a pre-retirement planning process which is strengths based and self-empowering for older employees, it is appropriate to consider a few other non-workplace prevention interventions EAPs might want to be aware of, to share with older workers facing retirement.

NON-WORKPLACE PREVENTION INTERVENTIONS VALUABLE FOR OLDER WORKERS

When working with older workers in preparing for retirement, there are several domains EAP practitioners should consider, as resource development or referral areas. Below are some key areas to develop for information and referral purposes, which can help older workers.

Peer Counseling

Peer counseling is another form of prevention where people help each other. Its uniqueness lies in the fact that trained women and men who are not professionals work with persons of similar age and experience. It has special appeal for older people who are reluctant to seek out professional services. The peer counseling concept facilitates the establishment of a special rapport that allows genuine supportive relationships to develop (Bratter & Tuvman, 1980).

Volunteering

In the aging community, older volunteers are used specifically to provide human contact to other older people who are confined and isolated. These consist of neighborhood or organizational support networks, i.e., Retired Senior Volunteer Program (RSVP), senior services' centers, councils on aging, nutrition programs, day-care and day-activity centers, and health and recreational programs. These in turn have generated other programs with more focused therapeutic potential, such as homemaker services, home health services, senior companion programs, friendly visiting, or a number of "telephone reassurance" projects (Hult, 1980).

In addition to receiving the benefits of volunteering for isolated older persons, it also fills a need for the older volunteer. In a study done by Tinsley, Colbs, Teaff, and Kaufman (1987) on the psychological benefits of leisure activities for older persons, a high percentage of respondents listed volunteerism as a satisfying leisure activity: 67% for men, 45% for women.

Computer Technology

Senior Net is a national computer program accessible to older adults who have computers as well as to senior centers with computers. Not only does it provide the challenge of acquiring computer skills, it is recreational, educational, and can be life-saving. An older woman, Eileen, who lives alone in North Carolina suffered a stroke and was able to get to her computer and send an SOS message to her computer counterparts in another state who were able to get her immediate help. She said of Senior Net, "I love it, I'm right up there with them (youngsters), I'm 'surfing' on my key board" (Davis, 1995).

Learning to Use Leisure Time

As discussed in preceding chapters, feelings of loneliness, boredom, and isolation can lead to stress and poor mental health. It is not necessarily the advent of retirement and all that accompanies it, including an abundance of leisure time, that produces these feelings. However, it may be a contributing factor.

There are as many ways to fill the leisure time that employment once occupied as there are individuals; some do it with ease, others struggle. People who have never traveled nor developed inwardly by engaging in satisfying hobbies prior to their 60s usually have a difficult time when they first try to "enjoy their leisure" (Meyer, 1980, p. 66). It takes learning and practice to acquire the necessary skills to travel easily and pleasurably or to play authentically so that hobbies and other activities can be genuinely satisfying rather then a time-filler/killer (Meyer, 1980).

Religion and Spirituality

While not considered a prevention program per se, religion and spirituality play an important role in the lives of most older adults in helping to promote good mental health. Maslow's view of human potential gradually expanded and he added a higher need level which he labeled self-transcendence. This manifested from his belief that human beings have a longing to transcend aloneness and feel a connection to others and to the cosmos (Maslow, 1968). The more years that people live, the greater the experiences they will have to reflect on, the greater the hunger they will have to explain themselves to themselves, and the deeper their need will be to justify their existence. Seniors have tended to maintain far greater involvement with religion than with other social institutions (Vayhinger, 1980).

Whether or not an older person holds a specific religious belief, many have some connection with spirituality and/or have spiritual needs that beg to be addressed, especially as they approach death.

From an earlier White House Conference on Aging, Moberg (1971, cited in Vayhinger, 1980) identified six areas of spiritual need: (1) socio-cultural needs, (2) relief from anxieties and fears, (3) a philosophy of life, (4) personality integration, (5) freedom from personal disunity, and (6) preparation for death. While employee assistance practitioners may not feel comfortable or competent in working with older adults in religious/spiritual matters, referrals to clergy can be made.

CONCLUSION

The greying of America and commensurate aging of the work force begs the issue for EAP professionals to have facility in address-ing the needs of older workers. This chapter has suggested that a strengths-based approach which emphasizes prevention interven-tions such as pre-retirement planning is self-empowering for older workers.

While there are sure to be many innovative approaches that EAPs can adopt as prevention/interventions regarding well being and pro-ductivity issues for older workers, the examples provided in this chap-ter give the reader an overview of a wide range of such services along with examples demonstrating how to integrate strengths concepts into existing programs.

By applying the strengths model, community building can be facili-tated amongst older workers, between them and the rest of the work force, as well as with the larger community. The workplace, then, can become a self-empowering venue for ensuring the strengths of older workers are optimized not only for personal benefit, but for collective well being.

REFERENCES

Achenbaum, A. (1978). *Old age in the new land.* Baltimore: Johns-Hopkins Univer-sity Press.
Atchley, R. (1976). *The sociology of retirement.* NY: Schenkman.
Atchley, R. (1982a). Retirement: Leaving the world of work. *The Annals of the American Academy of Policy and Social Science, 464,* 120-131.
Atchley, R. (1982b). The process of retirement: Comparing women and men. In M. Szinovacz (Ed.), *Women's retirement: Policy implications* of recent research. *Beverly Hills: Sage.*

Bergmann, B. (1971). The effect on white incomes of discrimination in employment. *Journal of Political Economy, 79*, 294-313.

Blank, R. (1982). A changing work life and retirement pattern: An historical prospective. In M. Morrison (Ed.), *Economics of aging: The future of retirement* (pp. 1-60). NY: Van Nostrand Reinhold Company.

Blau, F. (1984). Occupational segregation and labor market discrimination. In B.F. Reskin (Ed.), *Sex segregation in the workplace: trends, explanations, remedies* (pp. 117-143). Washington, DC: National Academy Press.

Bratter, B., and Tuvman, E. (1980). A peer counseling program in action. In S.S. Sargent (Ed.), *Nontraditional therapy and counseling with the aging* (pp.131-145. NY: Springer.

Burnham, L. (1985). Has poverty been feminized on Black America? *The Black Scholar, 16*, 14-24.

Commonwealth Fund commission on Elderly People Living Alone. (1987). *Old, alone, and poor: Technical analyses* (Report). Baltimore: Author.

Cory, E. (1993, June 10). *National Public Radio-Morning Edition*. Report on women's salaries.Washington, D.C.

Coyle, J.M. (1984). Women's attitudes toward planning for retirement. *Convergence, 2,* 120-131.

Daniel, P. (September/October, 1994). Learning to love growing old. *Psychology Today,* 61-70.

Davis, K. (1995, January 25). *National Public Radio-Morning Edition*. Report of Senior Net Services. Washington, D.C.

England, P., & Farkas, G. (1986). *Households, employment, and gender.* NY: Aldine Publishing Co.

Erikson, E.H. (1963). *Childhood and society,* (2nd Ed.). NY: Norton. *Federal Register.* "Notices," Vol. 56. No. 34 (Wednesday, February 20, 1991): 6860.

Faludi, S. (1991). *Backlash: The undeclared war against American women.* NY: Crown Publishing, Inc.

Gibson, R. (1983). *Work and retirement; aging black women–a race and sex comparison.* (Final report to the Administration on Aging). Ann Arbor: The University of Michigan.

Gould, K.H. (1989). A minority-feminist perspective on women and aging. In J.D. Garner & S.O. Mercer (Ed.), *Women as they age*: *Challenge, opportunity, and triumph* (pp. 195-216). NY: The Haworth Press, Inc.

Hall, G. (1980). Retirement planning: Suggestions for management. *Aging and Work,* (Summer), 203-209.

Hayes, C.L. & Deren, J.M. (1990). *Pre-retirement planning for women*: Program design and research. *NY: Springer.*

Hendricks, J. & Hendricks, C.D. (1981). *Aging in mass society: Myths and realities.* (2nd ed.). Cambridge: Winthrop.

Higgenbotham, E. (1986). We were never on a pedestal: Women of color continue to struggle with poverty, racism, and sexism. In R. Lefkowitz & A. Withorn (Eds.). *For crying out loud* (pp. 97-108). NY: Pilgrim Press.

Hult, H. (1980). The volunteer Connection. In S.S. Sargent (Ed.), *Nontraditional therapy and counseling with the aging* (pp. 119-130). NY: Springer Publishing Co.

Leonard, F. (1994). *Women and pensions* (Prepared for The Women's Pension Policy Consortium). WDC: Older Women's League.

Levitan, S., Mangum, G., & Marshall, R. (1976). *Human resources and labor markets*, (2nd ed.). NY: Harper and Row.

Maslow, A. (1968). *Toward a psychology of being*. NY: Van Nostrand Reinhold.

McKnight, J. (1992). Redefining community. *Social Policy*. 23, 56-62.

Meyer, G. (1980). The new directions workshop for Senior Citizens. In S.S. Sargent (Ed.), *Nontraditional therapy and counseling with the aging* (pp. 55-73). NY: Springer Publishing Co.

Mor-Barak, & Tynan, M. (1993). Older workers and the work-place: A new challenge for occupational social work. *Social Work*, *38*(1), 45.55.

National Center for Health Statistics. (1986). DHHS Pub. No.(PHS)87-1232, Washington, DC: Department of Health and Human Services.

Older Women's League (1990). *Heading for hardship: Retirement income for American women in the next century*. WDC: Author.

Perkins, K. (1992). Psychosocial implications of women and retirement. *Social Work*, *37*(6), 526-532.

Perkins, K. (1993a). Working-class women and retirement. *Journal of Gerontological Social Work*, *20*(1).

Perkins, K. (1993b). Recycling poverty: From the workplace to retirement. *Journal of Women and Aging*, *5*(1), 5-23.

Perkins, K. (1994). Older women in the workplace and implications for retirement: EAP can make a difference. *Employment Assistance Quarterly, 9*(3/4), 81-97.

Report on the Status of Midlife and Older Women. (1986, May). DC: Older Women's League.

Ross, H.K. (1983). The neighborhood family: Community mental health for the elderly. *The Gerontologist*, *23*(3), 243-247.

Sargent, S.S. (1980). *Nontraditional therapy and counseling with the aging*, (Ed.), NY: Springer Publishing Co.

Smith, J., & Ward, M. (1984). *Women's wages and work in the twentieth century*. Santa Monica, CA: Rand Publishers.

Social Security Bulletin (1993). Annual Statistical Supplement. Washington D.C.: Social Security Administration.

Sparr, P. (1986). Reevaluating feminist economics: "Feminization of poverty" ignores key issues. In R. Lefkowitz & A. Withorn (Eds.), *For crying out loud* (pp. 61-66). NY: Pilgrim Press.

Stone, R. (1986). *The feminization of poverty and older women: an update*. Washington, DC: National Center for Health Services Research.

Tinsley, H.E.A., Colbs, S.L., Teaff, J.D., & Kaufman, N. (1987). The relationship of age, gender, health and economic status to the psychological benefits older persons report from participation in leisure activities. *Leisure Sciences, 9*, 53-65.

U.S. Bureau of Census. (1994). *Statistical Abstract of the United States, 1994*. WDC: U.S. Department of Commerce Economics and Statistics Administration.

U.S. Bureau of Census. (1992). *Poverty in the United States: 1992*. Consumer Income, Series P60-185. WDC: U.S. Department of Commerce Economics and Statistics Administration.

U.S. Bureau of Census. (1990). *General population characteristics.* WDC: U.S. Department of Commerce.

Vayhinger, J.M. (1980). The approach of pastoral psychology. In S.S. Sargent (Ed.), *Nontraditional therapy and counseling with the aging.* (pp. 199-213). NY: Springer Publishing Co.

Weick, A., Rapp, C., Sullivan, P.W., & Kishardt, W. (1989). A strengths perspective for social work practice. *Social Work*, 34, 350-354.

EAPs and Critical Incident
Stress Debriefing:
A Look Ahead

David Plaggemars

SUMMARY. This chapter traces the development of critical incident stress debriefing; and, its particular use within EAPs. In addition to more traditional uses of CISD, applications of the model for workplace-based interventions addressing domestic violence, homicide, suicide, and department reorganization and change are offered. *[Article copies available for a fee from The Haworth Document Delivery Service: 1-800-342- 9678. E-mail address: <getinfo@haworthpressinc.com> Website: <http://www.Haworth Press. com>]*

KEYWORDS. Critical incident stress debriefing (CISD)

Critical incident stress debriefing (CISD) is a process which has received increasing attention since the early 1980's as a useful methodology in modifying the psychological distress resulting from exposure to traumas and crises. Although initially designed to assist emergency medical services and "first responder personnel," the process has more recently gained application in other contexts, including employee assistance programs.

Threats of company reorganization and downsizing, the realities of automation, the pressures of mastering new technologies, violence and harassment at the work place as well as economic pressures and

[Haworth co-indexing entry note]: "EAPs and Critical Incident Stress Debriefing: A Look Ahead." Plaggemars, David. Co-published simultaneously in *Employee Assistance Quarterly* (The Haworth Press, Inc.) Vol. 16, No. 1/2, 2000, pp. 77-95; and: *Emerging Trends for EAPs in the 21st Century* (ed: Nan Van Den Bergh) The Haworth Press, Inc., 2000, pp. 77-95. Single or multiple copies of this article are available for a fee from The Haworth Document Delivery Service [1-800-342-9678, 9:00 a.m. - 5:00 p.m. (EST). E-mail address: getinfo@haworthpressinc.com].

balancing work/family expectations are all realities which can create crises for employees. The purpose of this chapter will be to describe how critical incident stress debriefing can be used by EAPs to help employees cope with stresses that result from a variety of workplace-based traumatic situations, such as accidental deaths, departmental reorganization, acts of violence or serious workplace accidents.

To begin with, an historical perspective on the development of critical incident stress debriefing will be offered. Crisis and trauma concepts will then be elaborated, along with a discussion of the value of using group approaches to remediate stress-related symptoms which is the rationale for CISD. The steps of the CISD methodology will be explained and both traditional as well as non-traditional applications of the CISD process will be offered. Finally, emerging trends concerning the use of CISD in the workplace will be identified.

HISTORICAL DEVELOPMENT OF CISD

The systematic study of human responses to trauma traces its roots to the observation of military personnel during warfare. For example, the term "soldiers heart" described the response of Civil War infantry exposed to heavy combat and "shell shocked" was the analogous term applied to WWI combatants. Related to the latter mentioned phenomenon, experience showed that 65 percent of those affected who were treated close to the front lines were able to return to combat (Brown & Williams, 1918; Holmes, 1985; Salmon, 1991). Group debriefings were performed as a part of the Normandy D-Day operations and the experience of Vietnam combat veterans helped to define delayed stress reactions (posttraumatic symptoms) that could result from acute and cumulative combat situations (Hillenberg & Wolf, 1989). By virtue of research undertaken by the Israeli Defense Force conducted on the effectiveness of group debriefing immediately following combat experience, it was found that the use of such support services reduced the prevalence of post-traumatic stress by 60 percent (Breznitz, 1980; Holmes, 1985; Solomon, 1986).

The value of applying brief, immediate intervention to wartime trauma survivors began to be extrapolated to mass disasters, either natural (earthquake, flood, hurricane) or man-made (plane crash, urban fire). For example, the 1943 Coconut Grove night club fire in

Boston (with four hundred fatalities) afforded an opportunity to apply a group debriefing approach with mass trauma survivors (Caplan, 1964; Lindermann, 1944). More contemporary civilian catastrophes where group interventions have been applied to trauma survivors include terrorist activities such as the New York City fire bombing in 1990 (87 fatalities) and the Federal Building bombing in Oklahoma City (1995).

Perhaps mass transportation disasters have been most significantly associated with the development and use of CISD interventions, the first being a January 13, 1982 Air Florida crash which killed 76 passengers (Gwaltney, 1987; Yandrick, 1990). As the prototype for subsequent emergency response personnel rescue operation debriefings, Firefighter Captain Chip Theodore implemented CISD interventions for individuals involved with that airline crash rescue operation. This event is considered to be the "birth" of the CISD model as it is used today. Since its genesis with that particular airline crash, CISD has normatively been employed for rescue personnel involved in other mass transportation calamities involving airline, rail and bus crashes.

CISD technologies have also been used in large-scale community disasters. Natural disasters necessitating the use of CISD teams include the Mexico City earthquake, 1989; El Salvador earthquake, 1986; San Francisco earthquake, 1989; Los Angeles earthquake, 1994; as well as Hurricanes Hugo in 1990, and Iniki and Andrew in 1992.

With increasing use, it became apparent to administrators of organizations where staff were frequently exposed to traumatic events, that the regular utilization of CISD processes for affected staff could reduce workmen's compensation stress claims and related costs. As an example, growing awareness of the personnel retention benefits accruing from offering group trauma debriefings led to the creation of the Shock Trauma Center in Baltimore, which was the first major U.S. medical facility to provide CISD support services for its staff (Epperson-Se Bour, 1990).

Having reviewed some of the historical antecedents to the development of CISD, the next section will address crisis and trauma concepts which theoretically provide support for the technology.

CRISIS AND TRAUMA
AS UNDERGIRDING CONCEPTS FOR CISD

Crises

A crisis represents an acute emotional upset, loss of equilibrium, and an upset in a steady state which temporarily hinders one's ability to employ previously used problem solving capacities (Parad & Parad, 1990; Sussal & Ojakian, 1990). Crises can be situational and sudden (accidents, natural disasters), or maturational (a transition in the life process). Their etiology can be based on an acute or cumulative stressors (Van Den Bergh, 1992).

A crisis may have psychological impact for a few days or up to a few months. One's response will be based on constitutional as well as environmental factors and will go through stages, including: (a) exposure to a stressor, (b) experiencing disequilibrium symptoms and (c) establishment of an outcome (Mitchell & Resnick, 1981; Parad & Parad, 1990). By virtue of transiting through a crisis, one's outcome status can be at a level equal to, less or more than precrisis functioning.

Crisis symptoms are most often classified as physical, cognitive, emotional and behavioral reactions. Physical reactions include shock, nausea, fatigue, dizziness, and twitches. Cognitive symptoms are confusion, concentration problems, reduced attention span, problem solving difficulty, and memory impairment which may include amnesia. Emotional responses may manifest as anxiety, fear, loss, numbness, a sense of disbelief, identification with the victim, irritability, helplessness, and hopelessness. Finally, behavioral symptoms exhibited may include withdrawal or isolation, deteriorating ability to perform according to normal expectations, hyperalertness to one's environment, sleep and appetite disturbances and decreased sexual functioning.

Traumas

A traumatic event is more severe than a crisis (Gwaltney, 1987) has a more unpredictable onset (Figley, 1985), and as defined through the *Diagnostic and Statistical Manual of Mental Disorders, 4th Edition* (1994) involves an individual experiencing, witnessing or being confronted with actual or threatened death, serious injury or a threat to the physical integrity of self or others. By virtue of being traumatized, an individual's typical responses would include intense fear, helplessness or horror. Psychological symptoms associated with the trauma response include: (a) persistently reexperiencing the event (i.e., through intrusive thoughts or dreams), (b) avoidance of stimuli associated with the trauma as well as a generalized numbing of responsiveness (i.e., detaching from others) and (c) increased arousal (i.e., hypervigilance, sleep disturbances). Persons experiencing the above noted symptoms for more than one month, and to the point where social and occupational functioning are impaired, qualify for a diagnosis of post-traumatic stress disorder (DSM IV, 1994, p. 428; Hillenberg & Wolf, 1989). Individuals demonstrating those symptoms for less than one month but for more than two days, who also have dissociative symptoms such as an inability to recall important aspects of the trauma, can be diagnosed with acute stress disorder (DSM IV, 1994, p. 432).

As was true with responses to a crisis, one's trauma reaction will be affected by both innate characteristics (i.e., prior trauma experience) as well as factors idiosyncratic to the event (i.e., level of loss, destruction and duration of event (Wolf, 1992)). Other than the "sudden death" phenomenon, PTSD may represent the single most severe and incapacitating variation of human stress. Davidson and Baum (1986) postulated that four in ten Americans have been exposed to a traumatic event before the age of 30; of these, one in four developed PTSD.

INTERVENTIONS TO ADDRESS CRISIS AND TRAUMA RESPONSES

For both crisis and traumas, assistance to affected persons entails interventions which can enhance innate coping abilities such that one can return to, at least, a precrisis or trauma exposure level of functioning. It should be noted that it is possible for an individual to actually experience a crisis/trauma resolution such that one's level of functioning exceeds that of their prior functioning. However, it is also possible that without effective aid, a person could be negatively affected in being unable to function as they had previously.

The function of CISD is to take principles associated with treatment success for crisis and trauma resolution and apply them in a group setting (Van Den Bergh, 1992). This occurs by CISD interventions following a multistage process aligned with the normative phases of the crisis response; that is, addressing perceptions, responses and resolution. Through a group process, CISD employs early intervention, brief treatment, task centered and problem solving techniques which allow for a catharsis around having experienced a traumatic event.

The value of using a group CISD approach for treating trauma survivors is that it thwarts the normative tendency of such persons to isolate and withdraw; the ubiquitousness of that reactive behavior was even described by Freud (1920). In a group environment, the victim is joined with other survivors who were exposed to the trauma, whereby a certain "kinship" is established. Significantly, the group process can affirm that the survivors' disequilibrium and intrusions are not unique and that members are, in effect, "all in the same boat" (McFarlane, 1990).

INTRODUCTION TO THE CISD PROCESS

The effectiveness of CISD is derived from several aspects. Early intervention, often within hours after the trauma, is the best prevention against developing more difficult traumatic stress reactions. Prevention and early intervention efforts are clearly preferable to treating post-traumatic stress disorder (Duffy, 1979; Yandrick, 1990). While a strong emotional response to a trauma is not considered pathological, people's instinctive reactions (detaching, shock, intrusive thoughts) due to the intensity of the impact may inhibit the essential need for catharsis. Pennebaker and Susman (1988) concluded after their thorough review of literature that disclosure of traumatic events clearly reduces stress arousal. However, successful recovery from a trauma is based not only on the ability to express feelings but also on the ability to reconstruct and integrate the trauma using verbal expression (Mitchell & Everly, 1993; Pennebaker & Beall, 1986; Vander Hart, Brown, & Vander Kolk, 1989).

Throughout the CISD process, traumatizing material is gleaned through the structured flow of the group process, thus framing an accurate collective summary of the event. Borkovec et al. (1983) found that providing a structured environment for discussing troubling realities can reduce an individual's anxiety, as one's emotional confusion can be contained within a group structure. The CISD model provides a defined beginning and end, "superimposed upon a traumatic event representing chaos, suffering and . . . unanswered questions" (Mitchell & Everly, 1993). Combined with the support and education of the group leaders, traumatized individuals begin to reconstitute their healthy coping skills.

Mitchell and Everly outline several further goals for CISD. Among them are the following:

- Normalization of reactions to an abnormal event.
- Reassurance that the stress response is manageable.
- Reduction of the fallacy of uniqueness.
- Reduction of the fallacy of abnormality.
- Forewarning about possible future symptoms.
- Enhancement of group cohesion.
- Reinterpreting guilt and anger responses.
- Clarification of misconceptions or distortions of the event itself.
- Assessment of those who may need follow-up counseling.

STEPS OF THE CISD PROCESS

Critical incident stress debriefing is a group process for recently traumatized individuals, which can help to alleviate initial acute stress responses and accelerate the healing process. CISD ideally occurs within 72 hours of the incident. While offering CISD subsequent to 72 hours does not preclude its effectiveness, traumatized individuals benefit most while still experiencing the immediate impact of the event. Ideally, a CISD group would include 10 to 15 people, with 25 participants being the maximum group size in order for the process to be effective. Typically groups meet for two hours, with larger groups meeting somewhat longer in order to give all participants adequate time to discuss their reactions. More than one debriefing may be needed in order to cover all persons affected by a trauma.

Debriefings include at least one and preferably two mental health professionals, with one designated as the head facilitator. Trained peers assist the group facilitator by contributing to introductory and summary remarks as well as by giving timely feedback throughout. Peers also add credibility by offering strategic insight into the workplace culture and the affected co-workers.

The actual CISD process consists of seven phases. The *introduction phase* sets the stage for the subsequent phases of the debriefing. The mental health professional introduces himself/herself and the team members. The purpose, context and the process of the meeting are explained. Guidelines are explained, including the need for all participants to keep the content discussed within the debriefing confidential. Furthermore, it is clarified to participants that the debriefing is not a logistics analysis of the event. A supportive and nonjudgmental tone is established in order to reduce resistance, anxiety and to encourage mutuality among the participants.

In the *fact phase*, all persons are asked in a round-robin manner to introduce themselves, and their role during the incident. Since the facts are objective in nature, they are the easiest to discuss. This ideally facilitates a subsequent transition to more emotional responses. Through a discussion of the facts, a collective, realistic picture of the event is created.

In the *thought phase*, group members are asked, again in round-robin format, to state their first thought about the incident. For example, a CISD group member's first thought might have been, "I hope there aren't kids trapped in there." The thought phase represents a transition from the cognitive domain to the affective domain, thus preparing the participants for more personalized responses.

The fourth phase, *reaction*, is typically the most powerful in that participants are asked to recall the worst or most difficult part of the event for them. Typical responses could be, "I keep thinking . . . what else could I have done," or "I keep seeing that child's face . . . she was about my daughter's age." Eliciting responses during this phase is done in voluntary rather than round-robin fashion. If there are protracted silences the facilitator may rephrase a question or suggest what would be normal reactions to such a traumatic event (Mitchell & Everly). Often the thought and reaction phases blend together. By gradually putting words to what was most difficult for them, individuals begin to expose content that, if not dealt with, in all likelihood would prove most troublesome in the future.

The *symptom phase* redirects participants to consider the physical, emotional or behavioral symptoms they have experienced. The facilitator may stimulate the process by mentioning common stress-related symptoms which persons may have experienced since the trauma. By discussing them, the symptoms are normalized which hopefully may serve to reduce their frequency and intensity.

The *teaching phase* relays clear information on normative stress responses (what is considered a normal response to a trauma) and describes behaviors that assist individual recovery. It is typical to provide handouts to group members that underscore the content being imparted by the group leader. Healthy self-care habits are emphasized as normative responses to stress, as well as the phases people experience in the aftermath of a trauma. This information proves orienting, engenders a sense of self-control and encourages ongoing self-assessment during recovery.

The *re-entry phase* offers the opportunity to summarize, clarify particular issues, reemphasize key points and respond to remaining questions. It is also time for the facilitator to state any feelings that seem apparent but have not been expressed. At this point, sources for further assistance are identified. At the close of the debriefing the facilitators remain available for questions or further discussion.

Certain follow-up activities must then be considered. Post-debriefing feedback should be solicited from those who requested the debriefing, typically managers or supervisors. Specific recommendations regarding follow-up are suggested, including follow-up debriefings, chaplain visits, individual consultation, or referrals for counseling.

Finally, post-debriefing meetings, commonly called "debriefing the debriefers" are held (Talbot et al., 1991). Debriefers benefit by revisiting their responses in the meeting and learning from feedback and suggestions. Follow-up tasks may then be assigned (Mitchell & Everly, 1993).

Additional critical incident stress management and technologies include defusings and demobilizations. Of the two, EAP professionals are most likely to employ defusings. *Defusings*, also called defocusing, are in essence a shortened form of debriefing. Its application is more immediate (often within the first 24 hours) and is less intense due to a shorter involvement in the reaction phase. Furthermore, defocusings may preface a debriefing or may take the place of a debriefing. Defusings have three phases, (a) *introduction phase*, (b) *exploration phase*, which is a combination of the fact, thought and symptom phases of the debriefing and (c) *information phase*, which constitutes a blending of the teaching and re-entry phases of the debriefing. Defusings last approximately one hour.

Demobilization is designed to provide a basic amount of information about stress, to a large group of people, in a brief period of time. Typically demobilizations are performed after a large-scale disaster. It is comprised of a 10-15 minute stress education and stress management component and an ensuing decompression phase of approximately 20 minutes, allowing time to rest, eat and recuperate after having been on-duty.

In summary, the critical incident stress debriefing process facilitates the formation of a group support process led by trained mental health professionals, and possibly peers, wherein the presentation of factual data prepares the way for the expression of more emotionally charged content. Through the group process, participants are encouraged to share their thoughts, feelings and to engender peer support, while also becoming educated about posttraumatic stress reactions. Participants learn that their responses are not unique and that with both self-awareness and self-care, a sense of safety and security can be restored.

USES OF CISD BY EAPs WITHIN WORKPLACES

As was noted in a prior section covering the historical development of CISD, its initial utilization in the 1980's was for emergency response personnel exposed to trauma by virtue of rescue operation activities. Hence, the earliest use of CISD by employee assistance practitioners was related to traumatic events, as man-made or natural disasters, that affected workplace employees. In the following section, the author will describe CISD interventions implemented as an EAP practitioner for more traditionally deemed crises.

APPLICATION TO TRADITIONAL CRISES

Electrocution

A municipal department director called their EAP in response to an on-the-job accident. A forestry division worker had accidentally made contact with live electrical wires with a boom hoist resulting in severe electrical burns. A nearby crew negotiated a rescue amid arching live electrical wires, and the victim ultimately survived. EAP staff held a defocusing for those workers who were primarily involved and also the immediate supervisor who was the first responder. Questions asked by the facilitator during the debriefing allowed the participants to piece together the events in which they had participated. Predominant emotions expressed were great concern for the victim's well-being and a measure of unrealistic guilt for assigning that worker to that particular job. All participants appeared to be in a state of shock and disbelief and minimized their own role, and the risk they incurred. Facilitator efforts focused on normalizing the participants' reactions and presented education on traumatic stress responses to help the framing of possible symptomatic responses that might occur during the upcoming weekend. The meeting lasted for one hour.

A departmental debriefing was scheduled the following morning before normal working hours. The traditional CISD questions were asked. While the introductory and fact phase were completed, negative feelings about the victim squelched any further cathartic expression by the group. The facilitator then moved to the teaching phase, by generalizing typical post-trauma responses. This debriefing had paradoxically taken on the characteristics of a demobilization. In a follow-up defocusing four days later, the original crew was reassembled to assess their coping mechanisms. All reported intrusive thoughts, nightmares and sensory flashbacks, yet the participants reported that knowledge of "typical" traumatic symptoms was helpful in understanding their reactions.

Finally, office personnel who overheard the tragedy through radio dispatch and some staff whose spouses were line workers also requested intervention. The CISD model allowed for expression of their worst fear that a spouse or friend would be identified as the victim.

Homicide–Domestic Violence

Escalating domestic tension culminated in the homicide-related tragedy of a female employee at a large Midwestern accounting firm during the height of tax season. The victim was a well-liked, capable employee and her death triggered shock within the workplace, as well as the close-knit community in which she was involved. The shattered perception of the "perfect couple" proved unnerving to the victim's co-workers. Therefore, the firm's managing partners contacted the external EAP provider for help. EAP staff debriefed 30 co-workers, all female, who voluntarily attended the meeting. The following questions were asked: (a) Where were you when you heard about the incident? (b) What was your relationship to the murdered individual? (c) What was your initial thought when you heard about the murder? (d) What was the most difficult thing for you about the death? (e) What kind of symptoms did you experience? and (f) What is it like for you now?

It is noteworthy that at the time of the debriefing an investigation was underway which may have intensified participants' expression of feelings and reactions to the event. This murder was the first exposure to a violent death by all participants; hence, there were feelings of outrage, horror and unfairness. Facilitators provided education about trauma reactions and appropriate coping responses were also suggested.

Stabbing Death

The local owner of a nationally-franchised pizza restaurant called for assistance after a teenage employee died as a result of knife wounds received during a neighborhood fight. A debriefing was scheduled before working hours at the business located in a transitional neighborhood. Every employee and manager attended. The twenty youths' ages ranged from 16 to 19, and represented four cultural backgrounds. Two-thirds of the participants were male, one-third were female.

EAP facilitators followed the traditional format. After introductory comments, each participant was asked: (a) Where were you when you first heard the news? (b) What did you do upon hearing that news? (c) What was your response when you realized that your co-worker had died? (d) What is the worst thing about this? and (e) What is it like for you now?

Although anger and the desire for retaliation was expressed, the general tone of the group was somber. Feelings of shock, grief, and despair over the loss of a friend and co-worker prevailed. The adolescents gradually found words for their emotions and this appeared to have a calming effect. The store manager later reported that although tensions among staff remained high, the CISD process had quelled their urge to retaliate and had reinforced a stronger group cohesiveness. (Author's note: four months later, two employees were stabbed and seriously wounded just outside the debriefing site in what was described as a gang related attack on the employees.)

The above examples all suggest fairly traditional tragedies that called for CISD intervention. Within the next section, less traditional uses of CISD will be examined.

APPLICATION TO NON TRADITIONAL CRISES

Departmental Reorganization and Change

A request came to the EAP from a large Midwest manufacturing client to provide a group intervention for an organizational department undergoing downsizing. The company's payroll department, a cohesive, well-respected group, was being impacted by the prospect that many of their jobs would be eliminated due to contracting for outside financial services.

A strategy meeting was held with representatives from the human resources department and the vice-president of payroll. A departmental debriefing was arranged for the entire staff of 17 employees. Supervisors whose jobs were at risk attended. The vice-president was not invited.

Questions asked the payroll group included: (a) How long have you been with the company and how long have you been in your current capacity? (b) What is your current job function? (c) When and how did you first become aware of possible departmental changes? (d) What was your initial reaction to this information? (e) What was the worst thing about hearing the news at that time? (f) What responses might you be currently experiencing?

Most typical reactions included anxiety, fear, anger and hurt. Some employees, who had been with the company for many years, expressed a sense of betrayal. Other employees described gradually becoming detached and less motivated. The worst thing for many was the distancing that was occurring among members of a previously close-knit, award-winning department.

Interestingly, several members appealed for a rallying effort to "stand together" to fight for their existence. This "all in the same boat" tone engendered a certain sense of hope and cohesiveness.

The group decided they would like to meet again in three weeks to continue team building and to share ideas and plans for survival. On the day before this prescheduled meeting, a corporate decision was made to eliminate three-fourths of the current payroll positions. The EAP facilitator was notified of this development a few hours before the scheduled meetings. Since the purpose and direction of the meeting had now shifted, the EAP facilitator decided to postpone the meeting until employee notification could appropriately be communicated. Three days later the follow-up debriefing occurred. The facilitator explained the rationale for the postponement which was accepted by the participants. The meeting quickly took on the tone of a more traditional debriefing, targeting the direct impact created by the loss of their jobs. Team spirit dissipated and most members now verbalized the desire to look out for their own future. Many actually expressed relief that the uncertainty and waiting was over. Although the latest news was essentially bad, cognitive restructuring for many was already activated, making sense of this event and creating a need to reach some degree of closure with this latest development. Some speculated on other job possibilities within the organization, while others talked about their current efforts to develop outside job possibilities. Finally, in this meeting the group collectively confirmed their past identity as a worthy department that took immense pride in their work.

Hospital Staff Suicide

The personnel director of a mid-west community hospital reported that a clinical nurse manager had committed suicide. A debriefing was requested for all personnel including staff nurses, physicians, support staff and orderlies. Questions asked during this debriefing were: (a) Where were you when you first heard of the death? (b) What did you do when you first heard of the death? (c) What was your first thought when you became aware of the death? (d) What was your first response or reaction when you became aware of the death? (e) What was the worst thing about this for you? (f) What has it been like for you since the time of the death?

All employees were shocked, dismayed and some expressed a sense of betrayal that their leader had abandoned them. Initially, the group appeared somewhat guarded and cautious in talking about the nature of this death. It is noteworthy that the CISD process facilitated expression about suicide, in general, which ranged from judgmentalism to sensitivity toward the deceased, and respect of such a decision. No men were present at the debriefing. Intrusive thoughts about the victim, including sleep disturbance, was the most pronounced symptom expressed by group members.

This was an especially difficult event for many co-workers because the deceased was well liked and respected. She was perceived as possessing a strong character and often supported others during their time of need. Staff struggled with feelings of guilt and responsibility as they searched for apparent signs of potential suicide left by the deceased that they "missed." An interesting dimension of this debriefing was group processing about the spiritual outcome of suicide, for which there were strong and disparate opinions.

A requested follow-up session three weeks later was actually larger, perhaps, because of positive feedback from the initial session. Notably, co-workers who said little in the first session or who hadn't attended the initial debriefing were more verbal in their struggle to understand the event. They exhibited more anxiety and confusion than those who had participated in the initial debriefing; such persons were experiencing greater acceptance of the suicide.

FUTURE TRENDS IN CISD DEVELOPMENT AND USE BY EAP PROFESSIONALS

Having described various traditional and non-traditional uses of CISD by an EAP professional, it is now appropriate to conjecture about future trends related both to the development of CISD and its interface with employee assistance programs.

Future Trends in CISD Development

As critical incident stress management evolves, a number of adaptations within the CISD process itself are emerging. First, defusings may likely replace debriefings. While proven effective, the debriefing process is time consuming and often meets resistance from production-oriented managers in the work setting. Many plant managers, unfamiliar with CISD may be more receptive to a defusing which can be equally effective, and if necessary could lead to future CISD interventions.

Peer support will become increasingly important for the continuance and expansion of CISD interventions. Specifically, larger numbers of co-workers will receive training in the CISD process, thereby facilitating its acceptance and use.

Related to the above, we can anticipate greater participation in CISD debriefings from trauma survivors, trained as CISD team members. These individuals offer teams the strength of their experience, which can be both poignant and motivating for participants within a debriefing.

Another trend will be the growing multi-disciplinary composition of CISD teams. As CISD utilization spreads to a wider variety of workplace settings, use of a facilitator who represents the profession or job classification being debriefed (i.e., a nurse facilitator in a hospital setting) will maximize the impact of that team.

A final trend will be the proliferation of training materials about the CISD process which could be used for educating employees and managers about the benefits accruing from the use of CISD. For example, professionally produced documentaries could depict situations warranting CISD use as well as demonstrating the stages of the intervention process.

Future Trends in the Interface Between CISD and EAPs

Googins (1993) suggests that EAP's have been swept into the violence-prevention business as it has achieved "epidemic" proportions; to that extent, CISD is ensured ongoing use to address the aftermath, as well as prevention, of such events. Based on myriad factors including anger at job termination, cumulative stress engendered by downsizing, anxiety related to developing and maintaining technological skills and a work environment stressing the need to "do more with less," employee frustration is widespread. Additionally, an increasingly diverse workforce can create a reactionary response from some employees who see the influx of women and ethnic minorities as a threat to job security and the workplace status quo. Any one of the above factors, or a combination thereof, could serve as the precipitant for an episode of workplace violence.

By now it should be apparent that offering CISD interventions after episodes of workplace violence makes good business sense; however, less apparent may be the reality that use of the CISD process could defuse precrisis tensions. As was noted in the nontraditional CISD case examples section, CISD can be used to normalize the responses and minimize the reactions of displaced workers, and their employee peer survivors. Downsizing-based CISD groups not only engender mutual aid and peer support, they can facilitate a productive adaption to loss and change which may assist in the quest for another job or in transitioning into retirement.

CISD interventions can also play an important role in substantiating the ongoing need for EAP in an environment of managed care and national health care reform. EAP professionals, who deliver CISD services, can argue that they are saving money for their host organizations by reducing the need for traumatized employees to seek stress-related treatment. The CISD process empowers employees by encouraging emotional ventilation and participation in healthy self-care activities. In addition to lessening the need for protracted treatment, further savings can be realized through reduced disability claims, absenteeism and workmen's compensation litigation.

Another important future development is interorganizational collaboration between the Employee Assistance Professionals Association (EAPA) and the International Critical Incident Stress Foundation (ICISF). Jeffrey Mitchell, PhD, the ICISF founder has targeted the workplace as the emerging CISD frontier. In that regard, it would be important for both organizations to lobby for inclusion within health care reform proposals of tax credits (or related incentives) for early intervention and prevention programs such as CISD.

In a related vein, interorganizational collaboration between EAPA, EASNA, and the ICISF could engender outcome research on the efficacy of CISD. Although practice wisdom suggests that CISD is both efficient and effective, research efforts specifically focused on critical incident response have been minimal. EAP practitioners are in a pivotal position to challenge industry to underwrite CISD research, specifically to prove the effectiveness and cost-benefit savings accruing from its utilization.

Finally, the development and adoption of formal critical incident policy has been slow for most U.S. industries. The challenge for the EAP practitioner will be to influence industry to create policies that substantiate CISD use for workplace crises and traumas.Through such directed involvement, EAP professionals will ensure the vital role of critical incident debriefing in tomorrow's workplace.

REFERENCES

American Psychiatric Association (1987). *Diagnostic and Statistical Manual of Mental Disorders*. (3rd. ed., Rev.). Washington, DC.

Borkovec, T. D., Wilkenson, L., Folensbee, R., and Lerman, C. (1983). Stimulus control applications to the treatment of worry. *Behavioral Research and Therapy*, 21, 247-251.

Breznitz, S. (1980). *Stress in Israel*. In Selye, H. (Ed.) *Selye's Guide to Stress Research*. New York: Van Nostrand Reinhold Co.

Brown, M. W., and Williams (1918). *Neuropsychiatry and the war: a bibliography with abstracts*. New York: National Committee for Mental Hygiene.

Caplan, G. (1964). *Principles of Preventative Psychiatry*. New York: Basic Books.

Davidson, L., and Baum, A. (1986). Chronic stress and post-traumatic stress disorders. *Journal of Consulting and Clinical Psychology*, 54, 303-308.

Duffy, J. (1979). Emergency mental health services during and after a major aircraft accident. *Aviation, Space and Environmental Medicine*, 49, 1004-1008.

Epperson-Se Bour, M. (1990). Psychological crises services in the Maryland emergency medical services system. In H. Parad and L. Parad (Eds.), *Crisis Intervention Book 2* (pp. 209-226). Milwaukee: Family Service America.

Figley, C. R. (Ed.) (1985). *Trauma and its wake*. New York: Brunner/Mazel.

Freud, S. (1920). Beyond the pleasure principle. In J. Strachey (Ed.), The standard edition of complete *psychological works of Sigmund Freud* (Vol. 18). London: Hogarth.

Googins, B. K. (1993). The EAP and violence. *Employee Assistance*, 5(8), 16-19.

Gwaltney, H. (1987). Post-traumatic stress and the EAP response. *EAP Digest*, July/August, 57-60.

Hillenberg, J., and Wolf, K. (1989). Psychological impact of traumatic events: Implication for employee assistance intervention. *Employee Assistance Quarterly*, 4(2), 1-13.

Holmes, R. (1985). *Acts of War: The Behavior of Men in Battle*. New York: Free Press.

Lindermann, E. (1944). Symptomatology and management of acute grief. *American Journal of Psychiatry*, 101: 141-148.

McFarlane, A. (1990). Post-traumatic stress syndrome revisited. In H. Parad and L. Parad (Eds.), *Crisis Intervention Book 2* (pp. 69-92). Milwaukee: Family Service America.

Mitchell, J. (1983). When disaster strikes . . . The critical incident stress debriefing process. *Journal of Emergency Medical Services* 8(1): 36-39.

Mitchell, J., and Everly, G. (1993). *Critical Incident Stress Debriefing (CISD)*. Ellicot City: Chevron Publishing Corporation.

Mitchell, J., and Resnick, H. (1981). *Emergency Response of Crisis*. Baltimore: Robert J. Brady Co.

Parad, H., and Parad, L. (1990). Crises intervention: An introductory overview. In H. Parad and L. Parad (Eds.), *Crisis Intervention Book 2* (pp. 3-68). Milwaukee: Family Service America.

Pennebaker, J. W., and Beall, S. (1986). Confronting a traumatic event. *Journal of Abnormal Psychology*, 95, 274-281.

Solomon, Z. (1986). Front line treatment of Israeli combat stress reaction casualties: An evaluation of its effectiveness in the 1982 Lebanon War. *Israeli Defense Forces Journal*, 3(4): 53-59.

Sussal, C., and Ojakian, E. (1990). Crises intervention in the workplace. *Employee Assistance Quarterly*, 4(1), 71-85.

Talbot, A., Manton, M., Dunn, P. J. (1991). Debriefing the debriefers; an intervention strategy to assist psychologists after a crises. *Journal of Traumatic Stress*, 5(1), 45-62.

Van Den Bergh, N. (1992). Using critical incident stress debriefing to mediate organizational crises, change and loss. *Employee Assistance Quarterly*, 8(2), 35-55.

Vander Hart, O., Brown, P., and Vander Kolk, B. (1989). Pierre Janet's treatment of post-traumatic stress. *Journal of Traumatic Stress*, 2, 379-396.

Yandrick, R. (1990). Critical incidents. *EAPA Exchange*, 18-23.

Wolf, K. (1992). *Signs of Traumatic Stress*. Unpublished manuscript.

An EAP Approach
to Managing Organizational Downsizing

Dave Worster

SUMMARY. This chapter addresses multifaceted ways in which EAP professionals can be helpful related to organizational layoff realities. Suggestions are made pursuant to services appropriate for the downsized employees, as well as those remaining within the organization; "survivors" as it were. An appeal is also made for organizational communication processes which are inclusive and conducive to community building within the workplace. *[Article copies available for a fee from The Haworth Document Delivery Service: 1-800-342-9678. E-mail address: <getinfo@haworthpressinc.com> Website: <http://www.HaworthPress.com>]*

KEYWORDS. Layoffs, downsizing, organizational community building

INTRODUCTION

Dawn was just peeking over the horizon as the first employees approached the walk-in clinic to be greeted by a senior manager and an EAP staffer who gave them the bad news, yesterday was the last day of operations at this site. Concord (NH) Hospital was conducting a 10% reduction in force (RIF) and the clinic was expendable. Of the seven regular staff, one was re-assigned to the hospital and the rest were now without jobs.

[Haworth co-indexing entry note]: "An EAP Approach to Managing Organizational Downsizing." Worster, Dave. Co-published simultaneously in *Employee Assistance Quarterly* (The Haworth Press, Inc.) Vol. 16, No. 1/2, 2000, pp. 97-115; and: *Emerging Trends for EAPs in the 21st Century* (ed: Nan Van Den Bergh) The Haworth Press, Inc., 2000, pp. 97-115. Single or multiple copies of this article are available for a fee from The Haworth Document Delivery Service [1-800-342-9678, 9:00 a.m. - 5:00 p.m. (EST). E-mail address: getinfo@haworthpressinc.com].

Being laid off due to downsizing, right-sizing, merging, or restructuring, whether temporarily or permanently, is an unfortunate fact of life for thousands of workers across the country. Some segments of our economy were at one time believed to be immune from such pressures; especially healthcare. But, a rapidly changing system of payer regulations, fueled by needs to contain spiraling costs, has placed even healthcare organizations squarely in the struggle as well.

The effects are evident on those who have lost their jobs as well as those still working. Many of those laid off fear they will never find another job; retained employees have been left feeling insecure about their jobs, sensing that their work organizations will never be the same again. They have good reason to be concerned.

Layoffs have evolved into a major organizational cost-management tool over the last 10-15 years. Prior to that time, most layoffs were temporary in nature, resulting from seasonal changes or economic cycles, strikes and the like. But as corporate America moved more toward downsizing or reductions in force to improve the corporate "bottom line," as occurred in 47% of downsized companies (Medoff and Harless, 1996), to affect mergers/consolidations, or to increase productivity, the social contract and the sense of community between worker and employer has been altered, perhaps irretrievably. "Trust is a social resource that is destroyed by these attempts to conserve cash" (Medoff 1996, p. 141). Testifying before the House Democratic Policy Committee, Medoff suggested that the rate of permanent job loss has increased dramatically since 1980, even among well educated "white collar" workers. For example, male workers age 35-54 were twice as likely to suffer permanent layoff in the period of 1980-1993 than they had been in the previous 13 years. In 1990-1991, according to Medoff and Harless (1996), 86% of job loss was permanent. Among displaced workers from service-industry jobs, reemployment declined from 80% in 1990 to 66% in 1992. The Drucker Foundation reports that 3.5 million executives have lost their jobs since 1985 (Karpen 1996). Karpen also notes that re-engineering might result in as many as 25 million additional jobs, in the U.S. labor force, being lost in the foreseeable future.

Employees no longer expect, nor are they encouraged to consider, a career with one company. Workers have come to view themselves as management appears to, an expendable commodity. This belief persists despite the fact that finding adequate supplies of qualified workers is troublesome for many businesses. The resulting negative effects on worker loyalty have been documented many times (Raber, Hawkins & Hawkins, 1995; Samaha, 1993). The truth is that layoffs affect every employee in some way.

In the midst of this doom and gloom, EAPs are more frequently being asked to help downsized companies get back on track. Zemke (1996) notes that businesses are beginning to be aware that they need to re-create the sense of community that once existed at work. EAPs can play a crucial role in this process. This chapter proposes to examine the challenges that EAPs face in meeting that demand for the three constituencies involved in any layoff situation: the employees who are laid off, the surviving employees and managers who must carry on, and the organization itself where changing structures affect the organization's values and culture (Worster 1994). Examples from the author's EAP practice experiences will be added to illustrate certain points.

HELPING THOSE WHO ARE LAID OFF

A layoff is one of the most stressful and unnerving experiences a person can live through. The process mirrors that of any other loss: shock/numbness (even when there has been sufficient notice given), a flood of potentially chaotic emotions, and finally a re-balancing of the system (Temes 1992). In western culture, where egos are so intertwined with "doing," the blow to one's self-esteem can be intense. Regardless of whether the layoff had anything to do with personal performance, the tendency is to internalize the blame. Helping employees to move past taking the layoff personally is the first major challenge for EAPs.

Assisting separated employees can be complicated by an organization's perceived need for security following a lay-off. Whenever possible, EAPs should influence managers to allow sufficient time and space for appropriate processing of personal reactions. Shortcutting the grieving process leaves employees, both terminated and surviving, in a disconnected position and may foster the negative reactions feared by management. For example, in one hospital concerns for patient care and potential sabotage problems led to employees being informed of their layoff, escorted by security officers to their workstations to get personal belongings, and then escorted from the building. Many later complained they didn't get a chance to say good-bye to friends or explain what was happening. Some never did connect adequately with potential supports. Despite offering laid off employees generous severance packages, out-placement and other supports, employee anger around this process remained long after the event.

Communicating with Employees

Of the many important concerns in layoff situations, communication with workers has been noted by a number of authors (Seck 1992; Nail 1995) as being essential for both those who are laid off and those who remain. Seck (1992) suggests the communication tasks involved include designing advanced notification policies and methods to keep employees informed, planning with displaced workers for their unemployment, as well as anticipating and addressing the financial and emotional needs of the displaced workers and their families.

While employees (and others) need to understand the motivation behind the layoff in order to cope effectively, management may be reluctant to share information about impending changes due to fear of creating unnecessary distress and "unfocusing" employees from the job at hand. EAPs should encourage proactive information sharing, helping management to recognize that communication delays create the opportunity for rumors and other damaging misinformation to be spread throughout the organization, resulting in an atmosphere of mistrust and reduced credibility which makes management's task that much more difficult. An example of this proactive stance occurred in one company who's parent corporation decided to phase out local operations. The announcement was made to employees immediately, along with plans for how the employees would be supported over the 18 month phase out period. The company's EAP enjoyed an excellent working relationship with both employees and management. As part of the transition plan, management provided the EAP with the schedule for employee phase out. Thus, in addition to reaching out early, the EAP was able to anticipate needs as each employee's layoff approached. Virtually all the employees found new jobs with a minimum of life disruption. EAP involvement was seen by management as critical to this successful outcome.

The communication plan at one hospital included circulating several documents, among them a "commonly asked questions" pamphlet containing information such as: "Why has the hospital done this? Why now? Who made the decision? Who is affected? How were decisions about who was laid off made? What is the hospital doing for displaced employees? How much are we saving? Were there other alternatives explored?" Employees were also given a worksheet to help them explain the layoff to patients and visitors.

At the time of the layoff, hospital administrators held a "town meeting," open to all interested employees, to review the rationale for the layoff and answer questions. A written summary of the discussion was circulated for those unable to attend. These meetings continued on a monthly basis thereafter, providing a major source of information for employees about organizational developments. This effort has helped increase a sense of community among hospital employees.

Support to Terminated Employees

A second issue is understanding what support the organization will provide to laid off employees. Accessible information about possible severance packages (i.e., wages and separation pay, benefits coverage, etc.) provides employees a good place to start decision-making. For example, one hospital offered "early retirement" as a way of reducing the number of employees being involuntarily displaced. They also provided continuation of EAP benefits for one full year after the employee's separation as well as outplacement counseling.

Maximizing the information a displaced employee has at their disposal is crucial for good decision making. Given differing employee learning styles, providing information in a range of ways, such as group meetings, individual counseling and written materials or pamphlets, gives the most effective results. An example of written materials, created by Dahlstrom and Company (1994) for the New Hampshire Job Training Council, discusses such issues as: "Why is this happening to me?", "How is the layoff going to affect my family?", and "How am I going to pay my bills?", while providing practical resources and strategies for dealing with layoffs. EAPs can be the clearinghouse for this kind of information. One EAP used their monthly newsletter to do a series of articles related to downsizing, covering topics such as coping with change and locating resources to help laid off as well as remaining employees.

Employee Counseling Strategies

It is important for EAPs to remind both employees and managers that all changes, including layoffs, are a "feeling" as well as a "thinking" process (Bridges 1991). Understanding that feelings of shock, anger and/or grief are a normal and expected part of that process can help employees to adopt a more realistic outlook. Those in crisis often feel the need to talk about how they feel. Sharing with one's natural helping networks, i.e., family and friends, is the starting point for most people, even though they may be too emotionally close to help. EAPs can promote healing by considering the person's needs in context of her/his environment (Balgopal, 1989) as well as recognizing the need to move the process from mere ventilation (which can reinforce bad feelings and unhelpful responses) to a re-channeling of energy toward affirmative solutions. For example, an employee approached the EAP in a highly emotional, almost in a panic stricken, state following her layoff. She was unsure what to do, who to speak with; alternately angry, then tearful and terribly frightened. After a time, she was able to explore what some of her options might be. A follow-up call to her home the next day found her energized and focused on obtaining new employment. Within three days she had secured two part-time positions to replace the one she had lost.

Interventions with Older Laid-Off Workers

Quinn (1987) noted that older workers who are being laid off may require special EAP attention. Employees who are close to retirement may not receive as much sympathy or concern from their co-workers as younger workers, especially those with small children. While older workers may be financially better off than their younger counterparts, the crisis can be just as real and painful for them. Despite their proven track record, the older worker may wonder "who will hire me at my age?" Many businesses seem reluctant to hire older workers into "entry" level positions either because they are over-qualified or based on beliefs that they would be less productive due to lower pay scales than they had previously enjoyed. This creates a major dilemma for older workers who are neither interested in, nor prepared for, retirement (J. Lorden, personal communication, 1993).

Fostering Acceptance Attitudes in Terminated Employees

All persons have strengths which can be used in coping with setbacks and crises. The notion of resiliency includes willingness to learn, using one's self-esteem to bounce back from defeat or failure, recognizing and talking about feelings, maintaining a sense of humor and utilizing a personal philosophy which helps to provide meaning and direction to life (Goren 1988, p. 38). Frequently, strengths one is unaware of may be accessed in times of need. Reflecting back the person's strengths are very beneficial for maintaining and augmenting their coping capacities.

An employee's spiritual condition, including a belief in and connection to one's self, family and friends, and an optimistic view of the future, may be as important as his/her physical and emotional crisis coping mechanisms. Promoting connection or reconnection with the rituals attached to one's spiritual beliefs can be very helpful.

Employees may find it hard to believe that the loss of one job may lead to an opportunity to begin a new and exciting career. Many employees have remained in jobs where they were not happy because they were unwilling to risk loss of pay or benefits or feared inability to succeed in a new environment. Being laid-off can provide the person a chance to reassess interests and goals resulting in increased personal and professional satisfaction down the road.

HELPING SURVIVORS TO COPE

Typical Responses of Survivors

At the time a layoff occurs, most of our attention is focused on those who are losing their jobs. However, those left behind may be even more negatively affected. Many of these employees feel insecure, worried, betrayed and dismayed that their workplace contract (loyalty and service for job security) has been irrevocably altered. In addition, employees find themselves busy trying to adapt to new or added job functions, new reporting relationships and sometimes different work locations or shifts. They may begin to feel overwhelmed and underappreciated, frightened to speak out because "they'll be next," guilty over still having a job. Job performance and employee attitudes may be negatively impacted.

Most employees also fear further layoffs; the resulting uncertainty for employees is both real and palpable. For example, an EA professional recently reported that despite three and one-half years since an organizational downsizing, concerns related to layoffs were still being raised within employee stress management groups.

Frequently employees feel both anxious and powerless. They may be reluctant to expose their vulnerability by using EAP services. Instead, a "bunker mentality" may be adapted, meaning withdrawing to what is believed to be a protected position to "wait out the storm." In many companies, this strategy has been very successful over the years as employees have watched managers and management "fads" come and go. While a bunker mentality may leave one feeling safe, in reality they may be sitting directly in harm's way, similar to the turtle who becomes frightened and pulls into his shell in the middle of the highway. EAPs need to help employees understand that ongoing changes in our work organizations are permanent rather than transitory, thus requiring a more proactive coping strategy for the future.

Cognitive/Emotional Impact on Survivors

Communications from management concerning layoffs are directly related to survivors' subsequent reactions (Nail, 1995). When employees don't know why the layoff occurred, they tend to have exaggerated negative reactions, especially when the layoff has affected them significantly. Female employees may find transition further complicated if they become the primary "breadwinner" following their spouses layoff. The resulting tension of heightened fiscal concerns as well as changing household roles frequently results in EAP referrals related to role overload and conflict, not to mention exacerbated survivor guilt.

Ketchum (1988) notes that one of the "most overlooked" aspects of downsizing on employee reactions is a "loss of the future" in terms of what they had hoped for; or, expected. This can include loss of career path within the organization, as a frequent outcome of downsizing is to flatten organizational hierarchies. EAPs need to help employees move through the understandable grief reactions accompanying such loss (McConnell 1996; Fedorko 1989).

It is important to understand that the reactions employees may experience as the result of downsizing often resemble symptoms of depression, which may include difficulty in making decisions, decreased productivity, irritability or hostility, withdraw from others or extreme dependence, feelings of despair and hopelessness, chronic fatigue, unusual increase in errors, inability to concentrate, decline in dependability, susceptibility to accidents, increased tardiness and ab-senteeism, and lack of enthusiasm for work tasks (Hanus and Cooper 1993). There is growing concern nationally about the prevalence of depression in the workplace (Hanus and Cooper 1993). Such a trend may be attributed, in part, to increasingly unstable work environments.

Managing Downsized Employees

When considering how to manage surviving employees, it is first important for managers to accept that time and attention must be devoted to employee concerns; a task-oriented management approach will not be helpful. Scott and Jaffe (1991) and Jacobs (1988) contend that managers may be very tempted, given their own uncertainty and discomfort, to manage downsizing by attending to achieving fiscal goals at the expense of process considerations. EAPs should encour-age allowing employees and managers time to grieve losses and adapt to an ever increasing pace of change in order to facilitate transitions with a minimum of disruption. There is no "quick fix" in these situa-tions. Slow, steady strategies tend to bring the best results. It is also helpful, while not totally popular, to remind managers (and organiza-tions) that recovery and healing may take a long time. While some companies may hope to be "back on track" in a couple of months, a more realistic time frame might be 18 months or more. When manage-ment is not ready to accept the reality of a layoff's impact, they may become prone to quickly behaving "as if" everything is "back to normal." They may consequently become frustrated and disenchanted with employees who appear unable to "move on." Instead of blaming the victim, better outcomes can be obtained if managers take em-ployees "where they are at" rather than where they would like them to be (Seck 1992).

EAPs should encourage managers to use positive reinforcement techniques, finding employee successes and applauding effort as well as accomplishment. Managers should share information about future directions regularly and may even give their employees permission to use the layoff as an opportunity to innovate or take risks with areas of work they have wanted to improve. Additionally, managers can en-courage employee participation in planning processes, even if only to ask questions. The more employees are focused on what's ahead, the less they'll be dwelling on the past. Collaborating on goals and priorities can help eliminate time wasters, energy drainers, hard feelings and barriers to communication.

Management should encourage employees to use support services such as the EAP as well as their natural helping networks. Despite gains made in recent years regarding the acceptability of seeking counseling, many people still believe that, as adults, they should be able to solve their own problems. Seck (1992) notes that major concerns still exist around destigmatization of contacts with supportive services. Frequently employees believe counseling is only for "crazy people" or those "losing it," rather than understanding it as help in clarifying one's thinking and decision making. EAPs may find it helpful to downplay pathology and instead emphasize building on employee strengths. Enhanced employee comfort with EA services can result both in increased utilization as well as increased credibility with management.

Managers may also find it advantageous to have the EAP perform a critical incident stress debriefing (CISD) (Van Den Bergh, 1995). CISD has proven very helpful in layoff situations to help survivors realize they are neither alone nor abnormal in their reactions. In a hospital setting, the use of groups is additionally appealing because they mirror the changing emphasis from solo practitioners to a more team oriented approach. EAPs need to provide managers with education on CISD to avoid resistance stemming from time concerns or fears that CISD will exacerbate employee anxiety and despair by re-surfacing problems.

Other Supports for Downsizing Survivors

One of the most important coping strategies EAPs can encourage is for employees to share issues they are concerned with openly with their colleagues. This may take some courage, especially for those who fear that messengers with bad news and/or those who rock the boat will become the next persons laid off. In truth, withdrawal and isolation only ensure that things will not get better. Taking responsibility for becoming part of the solution rather than being part of the problem is also a way to channel the energy often associated with anxiety in useful ways. EAPs can help employees focus on and share the positives around them as well.

Longer term intervention might include offering ongoing informal support groups where employees can be encouraged to share how their day or week is going, to ask for help as they need it, and to share both stressful events and useful coping strategies. While personal issues might be revealed, generally the focus of attention is on work-related issues. For example, such a group began planning an employee picnic with their peers. While initially facilitated by EAP, the ultimate aim is for the group members to become leaders and provide self-help, mutual aid and peer support.

EAPs should encourage employees to understand that maintaining a sense of humor is essential to coping (Gorkin, 1994). Even black humor can be a very useful stress reducer. While managers may feel personally threatened by the proliferation of cartoons which malign management, such humor can actually help to create an emotionally safe work environment for employees. For example, one company formed an ad hoc "humor group" where interested members (both managers and employees) develop ways to lighten the environment. They recently sponsored an employee "Blues Brothers Review" which toured the company during "Beat the Blues" Day, handing out cookies and hot chocolate while dressed in fedoras and cheap sunglasses. Providing permission and opportunity for levity in the workplace can be beneficial to the organization as a whole.

ORGANIZATIONAL ISSUES FOLLOWING LAYOFFS

Altered Corporate Culture

Companies in the 1990's began to realize that all the organizational outcomes inherent in downsizing, etc., resulted in both intended and unintended changes in corporate cultures, which are not necessarily for the better. Zemke (1996) notes a nostalgia for the "good old days," especially the sense of a stable social contract between management and employees, the feeling of "family," which once existed in many companies. Today, many companies are attempting to create a sense of community to help them prosper in the future.

Traditional organizations have perennially taken a paternal approach to their employees, resolving problems and providing for members of the organization (Worster and Ricci, 1993). This created an environment where predictability and security were afforded workers in exchange for compliance. The "old" organization classically involved all decisions being made at the top. The "new" organization frequently sends a message which directly or indirectly states "you can't depend on us to take care of you." This means employees must rely more on themselves and their co-workers, assuming greater personal accountability and responsibility, with a resulting shift of decision making "closer to the action." Everyone now owns problem-solving, not just management, and employees will most likely be evaluated in the future based on their problem-solving performance. At the same time, employees need to feel it is acceptable to make mistakes rather than feeling they must constantly strive for perfection.

Another area of corporate culture warranting EAP intervention centers on developing new norms around conflict and criticism. The organization needs to be open to criticism, seeing it as a way to illuminate areas for improvement as opposed to "trouble making." This implies helping the organization to move from an environment where open conflict is not acceptable to one where disagreement and dialogue are routine. Conflict is a normal part of change, in itself neither bad nor needing to be managed. Employees need to learn how to "disagree without being disagreeable" and how to negotiate "win-win" solutions. Those who have a hard time establishing work boundaries and saying "no" need to accept that they can no longer be "all things to all people" (Worster and Ricci, 1993).

Altered Workforce Demographics

In some cases, employees who are valuable members of the organization may *choose* to leave as a result of downsizing. For example, in one hospital department all of the master's degree prepared employees either opted for early retirement or were laid off (based on less seniority), which rendered the department both leaderless and without experienced staff to carry on in the face of mounting organizational demands. In some organizations, serial layoffs have profoundly altered the make-up of the workforce over time, bringing new challenges based on employee life stage and tenure within the organization. For example, the average age of the remaining employees at one defense-related organization is over 50 years old, meaning that 95% of all employees qualify for early retirement. Consequently, many experienced workers may be encouraged to leave with potentially devastating organizational effects. EAPs can be beneficial in addressing and healing the real and perceived wounds caused by the transition of organizational structures and cultures.

Performance Evaluation Imperative

Workplaces restructured by downsizing need to strongly consider placing more emphasis on performance evaluation. Lack of a workable performance management system can create unintended consequences both in terms of workforce changes and organizational structure. For example, in one company the original layoff plan called for managers to review the performance evaluations of all employees and make recommendations for layoffs based on retention of high performers. Administrators found, however, that annual performance evaluations did not accurately reflect employee work habits, forcing the layoff to be conducted on basis of longevity instead. This resulted in some very productive employees being laid off, while less productive but senior employees remained.

Johnson notes that "the traditional EAP concern for job performance is no longer the primary organizational focus of EAPs . . . (which) . . . may result in EAP not being the device that comes to organizational leader's minds when making decisions about how to alter an organization's future size or structure" (Johnson, 1995, p. 25). Returning to our core technology, EAPs should emphasize the importance and larger implications of the organization's performance management efforts as well as the EAP's role in making it work. Support for managers and supervisors through training and consultation is critical to this process.

An element of improving the performance management process involves enhancing management's understanding and use of constructive confrontation techniques. For example, a recently hired manager came to the EAP because employees were exhibiting chronic performance problems which had not been addressed by previous managers. The EAP and manager met regularly for a time to review ways to achieve a balanced approach, helping her to catch employees "doing something right" as well as coaching and counseling their poor performance. With her persistent efforts, performance and morale improved measurably over the next few months.

Creating a New Vision

Another important issue is the need to create a new "vision" for the organization post downsizing (Scott and Jaffe 1991). For example, in a hospital coping with layoffs, the EAP collaborated with senior managers and organizational development staff to identify and instill organizational values and initiatives which would assure the future success of the organization (Worster and Ricci 1993). Among the critical elements identified were a sense of ownership and pride on the part of employees, a sense of empowerment and control, demonstrated respect and appreciation, a vision for the future and an understanding of change processes, a commitment to "quality" and a willingness to take risks. Challenges included learning to deal with rapid internally and externally driven changes, accepting ambiguity, accomplishing an increased volume of work with fewer employees and orienting a new top management team. An atmosphere of trust predicated on internal accountability, including a need to be genuine in evaluating and implementing new models of service delivery, needed to be developed within the organization. It demanded the organization be a community where the various component parts recognized their interdependence and worked in new and more cooperative ways. Possessing the skills and ability to interact effectively and build relationships was recognized as a critical factor to organizational and personal success.

Developing Community

In order for this sense of community to develop, organizations need to create an environment where learning and growing become valued behaviors. Malcolm Knowles (1973) coined the phrase *androgogy* to describe an educational approach whereby adults, invested in their personal beliefs and behaviors, could be motivated to change if an atmosphere of safety and trust were established. EAPs are natural partners for organizations in this process.

Heenan states "line managers have neither the training nor the perspective to see beyond the segment . . . they . . . run" (Zemke, 1990, p. 33). By virtue of their larger organizational perspective, EAPs can be an effective conduit to provide education and coaching. For example, in one organization the EAP collaborated with in-house library services, conducting periodic literature searches to locate useable references and distributing them throughout the organization. This effort not only enhanced EAP credibility with managers at all levels, it resulted in the EAP being viewed as an on-going part of the solution.

EAPs need to meet managers on a more personal level (Ersner-Hershfield & Second, 1994). As an example, the EAP sponsored an open-ended group that provided a forum for managers to speak of their personal distress in a safe environment. Despite new organizational norms, many felt they could not show their concerns for fear of appearing disloyal to the organization and thus putting their own jobs at risk.

Mourning (1996) notes another strategy to enhance the sense of community involves expanding traditional volunteer activities to include new, project based activities providing community benefit. "At a time when massive layoffs and major restructuring have shattered morale . . . our transition toward community outcomes has lit small fires of passion throughout the institution" (Mourning, 1996, p. 28-29). Implemented in a hospital setting, she found that the process reminded people about why they had gotten into their profession in the first place and developed a positive connection to community outcomes.

Collaboration for Community Building

Developing and directing organizational responses to layoffs is not a task which the EAP should undertake by itself. Thus a major challenge is finding and/or developing collaborative relationships upon which to build enhanced services. At Concord Hospital, we focused on the interactions among EAP, Human Resources and Management/ Organizational Development. Each department has unique tasks and responsibilities; however, there are also considerable areas of overlap. Employees might approach HR staff or the OD trainers with issues of a personal nature; while, the EAP might be asked to intervene in workgroup problems or troubles with a manager, leading to periodic concerns over "turf" encroachment. To address this issue, the EAP, HR and OD managers met with senior management to develop a vision for how these organizational departments might work most effectively together. Clarifying the boundaries of confidentiality as part of developing a template for communication and cooperation amongst those three organizational entities, was particularly helpful.

An outcome of this collaboration between EAP, OD, and HR was the creation of a mutual mission statement to partner with each other to "solve and prevent performance problems." HR does this in the realm of employee to employer disputes, OD in the realm of work group concerns and EAP in the realm of personal problems impacting employee performance. We agreed, within the bounds of confidentiality, to share information regarding situations which had direct implications for another component's primary area of responsibility. HR and OD had a somewhat easier time with this given they are not professionally bound to confidentiality in the same way EAPs are. Still, we were able to develop a language respectful of client's privacy in the context of a communication system which allows for the sharing of limited information on a need-to-know basis. This process is akin to providing periodic reports on EAP activities. Within this collaborative structure, the EAP can work with OD and HR to become the "eyes and ears" of the organization, observing trends and evaluating both the effectiveness of management interventions and the need/direction of future responses. Most companies find this type of feedback invaluable.

Workplace Violence

A discussion of organizational responses to layoffs would be incomplete without some mention of the issue of potential violence. Nail (1995) suggests screening of job candidates prior to employment to assess potential for violence. Proactively obtaining EAP assessments for employees who are being laid off, identifying those possibly at risk and preparing appropriate interventions (CISD or some other form of support) could be recommended. Support for managers, whether provided by the EAP or other internal/external resources, in the form of training on managing termination meetings, handling various employee reactions and conducting themselves in ways which will not trigger workplace violence is crucial. As preparation plays a major role in successful outcomes, managers may find it invaluable to role play various scenarios with the EAP to enhance conflict prevention skills.

THE FUTURE FOR EAPs AND DOWNSIZING

While some sources in our country have suggested that the trend toward mergers and downsizing has slowed, a brief search of the Internet located more than 15,000 responses to the word "lay-off," including weekly layoff reports. Not only does downsizing continue at an epidemic pace, downsizing has been "normalized" and is now a part of our culture. Moving from job to job, from career to career, has become more the norm than the exception. Cultural changes including an increasing number of women and people of color in the workforce, an explosion of technology and increased use of part-time or temporary employees by companies, have created new models for work. There has been a profound effect on the social contract between employers and employees. We are now in an economic revolution which rivals the shift from agriculture to industry which occurred during the 19th century.

Eisenberg (1996) suggests that stress is a function of the amount and pace of change we're experiencing at any given time divided by the coping skills available to us. This equation implies EAPs can best assist employees by maximizing the coping skills available to each workplace constituency. EAPs must help to transform the workplace from a scene of chaos and distress to a place where there is the opportunity to create a new sense of community. Employees cannot be optimally productive without a safe environment. EAPs need to encourage organizations to adopt humane HR policies where people become more important.

EAPs cannot accomplish this mission by themselves. We need to become ever more mindful of the natural alliances which we can form with both formal and informal organizational leaders in order to have a greater role in organizational decision making. EAPs need to continually assess and nurture relationships with both employees and employers, emphasizing our strengths and being willing to risk disagreement in the name of ethical and appropriate service delivery.

Moving into the millennium, the need for EAP services will grow as more organizations realize their survival depends on how well they are able to help their employees cope with the ambiguity of today's world while remaining focused on the organizational tasks at hand. EAPs need to help develop a new sense of community in the workplace through connecting employees and management in more creative and productive ways.

At the same time, EAPs must also pay close attention to our own well being, physically as well as mentally. The work of dealing with layoffs, as well as many other workplace concerns and crises, can be especially draining. Failing to take appropriate care of ourselves leads to burnout and ineffectiveness. EA professionals are employee role models for their organizations and must take great care to "walk the talk."

Finally, we must educate employees and management, not only about humane approaches and strategies for addressing workplace problems, but also about who we are and why we are an essential and effective component of any organization's benefit package.

REFERENCES

Adams, J., Ed. (1986). *Transforming Leadership: From Vision to Results*, Miles River Press.

Balgopal, P. (1989). Occupational social work: An expanded clinical perspective. *Social Work. 34 (5)*. 437-442.

Bridges, W. (1991). *Managing Transitions*, New York: Addison-Wesley Publishing.

Dahlstrom and Company (1994). *Surviving a Layoff: Coping with the Emotional, Financial, and Job Hunting Stresses of Unemployment*. Concord, New Hampshire: NH Job Training Council.

Eisenberg, Howard (1996, March). Stress management: Preventing burnout and empowering patients. Presentation given at Brattleboro (VT) Retreat Continuing Education Workshop.

Ersner-Hershfield, S. & Segond, G. (1994, April). Let's not forget the messenger: The toll on those who wield the axe. *EAPA Exchange*.

Fedorko, S. and McKinney, M. (1989, June). Last whistle. *Employee Assistance*. 12-17.

Goren, M. (1988, Nov./Dec.). Interview with Fredric Flach, MD: The resiliency hypothesis and employee assistance counseling. *EAP Digest*. 35-38.

Gorkin, M. (1994, April). Laughing in the face of layoffs: The dark and light sides of job loss. *EAPA Exchange*. 22-23.

Hanus, R. & Cooper, C. (1993). Down time: A worksite guide to understanding clinical depression. Omaha, Neb.: Wellness Councils of America.

Jacobs, D. (1988, April). Maintaining morale during and after downsizing. *Management Solutions*. 5-13.

Johnson, A. (1995). Employee assistance programs and employer downsizing. *Employee Assistance Quarterly*, 10 (4). 13-27.

Karpen, M. (1996). Career crossroads, ideas and inspiration for your work/life journey. *Work World*. [http://www.authorweb.com/karpen/]

Ketchum, G. (1988). Mergers, downsizing, and layoffs: Managing employee reactions. *EAP Digest. 9 (1)*. 41-45.

Knowles, M. (1973). *The Adult Learner: A Neglected Species*. Houston, TX: Gulf Publishing.

Lorden, J. (1993, June). Personal correspondence.

McConnell, C. (1996). After reduction in force: Reinvigorating the survivors. *The Health Care Supervisor. 14 (4)*. 1-10.

Medoff, J. & Harless, A. (1996). *The indebted society: Anatomy of an ongoing disaster*, Boston, Little, Brown and Company.

Mourning, E. (1996, September). Managed care, healthy communities and the new healthcare foundation. *Fund Raising Management.* 24-31.

Nail, A. (1995). A role of EAPs in the downsizing process: A review of the literature and a model for practice. *Employee Assistance Quarterly,* 11 (2), 15-35.

Quinn, G. (1987, March/April). Surviving layoff. *EAP Digest.* March/April. 31-34.

Raber, M., Hawkins, M., & Hawkins, W. (1995). Organizational and employee responses to surviving the downsizing. *Employee Assistance Quarterly. 10 (4).* 1-11.

Samaha, H. (1993, Spring). Helping survivors of downsizing stay on track. *The Human Resources Professional,* 12-14.

Scott, C. & Jaffe, D. (1991, May/June). From crisis to culture change. *Healthcare Forum Journal.* May/June, 33-41.

Seck, E. (1992). Social work interventions with displaced workers. *Employee Assistance Quarterly. 7 (4).* 77-100.

Temes, R. (1992). *Living With An Empty Chair: A Guide Through Grief,* New York, New Horizon Press Publishers.

United States House of Representatives (1996, March 11). Report to the House Democratic Policy Committee. *Downsizing the American Dream.* {http://www. house.gov/democrats/research/downsize.html}

Van Den Bergh, N. (1992). Using critical incident stress debriefing to mediate organizational crisis, change and loss. *Employee Assistance Quarterly. 8 (2).* 35-55.

Worster, D. & Ricci, R. (1993). Employee assistance programs in partnership with management/organizational development programs at Concord Hospital. Unpublished paper presented at Employee Assistance Professionals Association Eastern District Conference, Williamsburg, VA, July 12, 1993.

Worster, D. (1994, April). The survivor: Looking ahead after layoffs. *EAPA Exchange.* 16-17.

Zemke, R. (1990, November). The ups and downs of downsizing. *Training.* 27-34.

Zemke, R. (1996, March). The call of community. *Training.* 24-30.

Organizational Development:
An EAP Approach

Myron Beard

SUMMARY. This chapter traces the development of organizational development as a workplace intervention approach which can be helpful for EA professionals specifically trained in its methodologies. Examples of the use of OD techniques to assist in "coaching" organizational top management, and the implications of that kind of team building for the organization are shared. *[Article copies available for a fee from The Haworth Document Delivery Service: 1-800-342-9678. E-mail address: <getinfo@haworthpressinc.com> Website: <http://www.HaworthPress. com>]*

KEYWORDS. Organizational development, succession planning, team building

THE NEW ORGANIZATIONAL FRAME

Unparalleled organizational changes characterized the past decade for U.S. companies and industries. There was a focus on increasing the efficiency of processes and people to maximize profits and reduce expenditures. These efficiency initiatives included downsizing to reduce layers of managerial fat; re-engineering to reduce product process steps and time to market; restructuring to create greater turnaround in decision making; and the total quality movement which

---

[Haworth co-indexing entry note]: "Organizational Development: An EAP Approach." Beard, Myron. Co-published simultaneously in *Employee Assistance Quarterly* (The Haworth Press, Inc.) Vol. 16, No. 1/2, 2000, pp. 117-140; and: *Emerging Trends for EAPs in the 21st Century* (ed: Nan Van Den Bergh) The Haworth Press, Inc., 2000, pp. 117-140. Single or multiple copies of this article are available for a fee from The Haworth Document Delivery Service [1-800-342-9678, 9:00 a.m. - 5:00 p.m. (EST). E-mail address: getinfo@haworthpressinc.com].

117

seeks to reduce scrap and returns while producing more efficient and effective products. While all of these trends have been both necessary and important, they have attended more to controlling costs and maximizing efficiencies than to expanding and growing businesses.

The rate of change in the competitive marketplace has many suggesting that the future will look substantially different from the past, even suggesting that forgetting the past will be imperative for future success. For example, from mid-1995 to 1997, the Dow Jones Industrial Average climbed more than 2000 points, a 33% gain. This period, and that which preceded it, marked the greatest expansion of U.S. business over any comparable period of time. Enhancing the stock market's growth, the dollar remained strong against other international currencies, especially the mark and the yen. Unemployment was steady at a very low 5.5%. The federal reserve has exercised a tight reign on inflation while keeping interest rates at 20-year lows (Securities Data Company, 1997).

These financial milestones are further supported by a record number of mergers and acquisitions, both domestically and worldwide. According to Securities Data Company (1997), more than 10,000 mergers and acquisitions occurred in 1996, representing more than $660 billion in the U.S. alone. Worldwide merger and acquisition activity accounted for over $1 trillion. The financial activity is staggering (Securities Data Company, 1997).

The deregulation of several industries, globalization trends and the availability of money have accompanied and fueled these activities. The relatively unrestrained anti-trust and regulatory environment in which old industries (e.g., utilities) are opened to competition has encouraged consolidation and the creation of new market space. A global economy in which companies often find themselves required to become big in order to compete, either by acquiring or being acquired, in addition to a supply of readily available money, due to falling interest rates, has encouraged rapid expansion. These forces have served as the determinants of this high level of financial activity. The need to make strategic changes as swiftly as possible to increase the competitive edge is central to staying viable and growing in the future.

Many believe that these financial markers indicate that business growth has reached the limits of incrementalism. In order to compete in the future, existing methods such as speed and flexibility, and a focus on cost and quality, will not create a competitive advantage. Rather, to be competitive, companies must reinvent existing competitive space, challenging the very trends and concepts which have made them successful (Hamel and Prahalad, 1994). This must begin with radically changing the thinking and action of managers and helping them challenge existing organizational points of view. Needless-to-say, this represents a huge challenge and threat to the existing methods of doing business for many, if not most, organizations. These challenges are accompanied by anxious ambiguity as well as insecure and often undirected momentum into an unknown competitive future. An analogy is one of driving rapidly, headlong, into a fog while simultaneous trying to change the tires or even the engine, hoping both to keep ahead of the competition and reach a desired, but uncharted, target.

In order to be of greatest service to work organizations and employees affected by rapidly changing business and economic conditioning, the EAP practitioner needs to keep abreast of business trends and the impact of those trends on individuals within an organization. This article addresses one pathway for the EAP practitioner to pursue in helping to serve organizations in flux; that is, to become involved with organizational development practices within a company. The EAP practitioner desiring to broaden his/her skills or to develop competencies in more organizationally-based interventions, such as organizational development (OD) must begin with an understanding of contemporary business, the organizational context, and the personal competencies necessary to successfully navigate and negotiate in today's business world. The scenario which follows depicts a need for intervention with a manager, which could easily be an example of a context for OD work by an EA professional.

CASE STUDY #1–FAILURE TO FORGET THE PAST

A senior level executive in a mid-western manufacturing company was a loyal company employee. His loyalty had been rewarded by successive advancements from Process Engineer to Plant Manager to Vice President. He was rigidly bound to the style of management which had led to his success. His style was characterized by centralized decision-making and a leadership style that was dictatorial and autocratic. He was known for his "passion" which was often a thinly veiled rationalization for angry outbursts. Nonetheless, he was a strong technical and financial thinker who had a track record for success in every subsidiary he had managed. His managerial behavior was characterized by an obsession with cost cutting and cost control. In every new situation, he led with deep personnel cuts. He justified this approach by pointing to increased profitability. Upon a closer look, however, it was noted that while his units were profitable, they failed to grow in terms of revenue, market share and new product development. The profits were due to decreased costs, not to an emphasis on growth. When it became apparent that competitors were outpacing this company, the failure to seriously develop a growth strategy began to erode the company's marketplace presence and revenues. The executive held steadfastly to his cost-cutting methodology. When new management changes occurred, his singular, antiquated approach was challenged and he was "retired."

In regard to the above case study, an EA practitioner could have been engaged in an OD intervention with the senior manager by assisting him in altering his management approach. Building upon his existing strengths would have been a way to proceed in this kind of OD endeavor. To be successful in that role, an EA practitioner would need to move from a "troubled employee" perspective, to a strengths-based, enhanced performance approach. An understanding of motivational styles, an individual's competencies and strengths, as well as factors associated with resistance to change, are key directions to pursue in working with managers around their management style.

In considering management styles which may be most optimal for the future, the section below seeks to elaborate traits considered helpful for managers to demonstrate, within a dynamic business environment.

THE NEW ORGANIZATIONAL LEADER

Leaders of the future need to meet the challenges of a competitive world vastly different from that of the past. The template for leadership is rapidly changing and will continue to change dramatically if organizations are to remain economically vital and vibrant. Characteristics such as good interpersonal skills, high intellectual capacity, in-depth technical knowledge and the ability to implement major organizational initiatives have been considered adequate for success in the past. These same characteristics are now seen as essential for entry into the new organization, but not for optimal management success. New skills in the areas of cognitive, behavioral and interpersonal functioning would have to be honed.

COGNITIVE

Traditionally, leaders have achieved success by managing and improving processes that are already in existence. In this sense, they have functioned much more as editors than writers by incrementally increasing efficiencies and improving existing knowledge. The need to be responsive to customer requirements and to produce quality goods and services has been critical for success. However, future success will be more affected by the capacity for creativity and innovation.

The thinking of the future will be like that of a writer in front of a blank page seeking to anticipate what will provoke readers' interests or to lead the reader into new and different worlds of thinking. Strong analytic and tactical problem-solving skills are of little use when the problem area is ill-defined or undefined. What the future requires is the cognitive ability to be innovative, reactive and inventive, anticipating and/or creating customer need. In addition, it will be necessary to learn rapidly and to utilize what one has learned to modify, clarify and redirect initiatives. This requires having high intellectual capacity in addition to having capacities for managing and embracing ambiguity, inventing the future, and stimulating the thinking of others. Challenging what is already known is important; and paradoxically, particularly if the known has been successful. In essence, one must move beyond strategy with knowns, to envisioning that which does not now exist.

BEHAVIORAL

Changing the thinking of future leaders is only effective insomuch as it is manifest in behavior change. To think progressively, but act in a status quo frame, is a mismatch that can confuse and disrupt. Without doubt, the courage to pursue bold and provocative ideas while mobilizing them into action is central to changing the organization.

American organizational behavior has been characterized by activity; and, too often, reactivity. The future manager, however, must transcend this reactive, responsive behavior and begin boldly stepping out into the unknown. To make expeditions into the marketplace to investigate, explore and learn is an essential first step. To take risks in the absence of sufficient knowledge and to feel, at times, as if one is in a free fall, is all part of the new leadership behavior. This may entail taking actions contrary to prevailing organizational sensibilities and becoming perceived as a rebel or eccentric. One's grounding, for this nonnormative behavior is based upon the knowledge that what has been done in the past does not necessarily predict to what will be a successful future. Change is happening too rapidly. Being a "good corporate soldier" will be associated with behaving according to a rapidly antiquated status quo.

INTERPERSONAL

The ability to leverage talent across the organization will be essential to grasping the opportunities of the future. Leveraging talent includes focusing employees on the highest and best use of their abilities, in order to move the organization forward. It is an active process of raising the bar and providing developmental and training opportunities which maximize employee potential. The past decade has witnessed change from a centralized, hierarchical, top-down management style to one that is more decentralized and team-based. Team-based organizations can be problematic in not providing enough direction and failing to focus on the "big picture" of which a group's activity is a component part. The new leader must work to increase communication and work activity across the entire organization to capture or create opportunities. The "not invented here" and "private ownership" behaviors have no place in the organization of the future.

Leaders must go beyond concepts like effective delegation, holding others accountable and empowerment to become inspirational provocateurs of aspirational behavior in others. This includes challenging others to create linkages throughout the organization for hidden or unrealized opportunities; to mentor, coach and encourage others to regularly take risks, behave and think in a visionary, forward-thinking manner; to reward new endeavors, *even when they fail*; and to create a learning, thinking environment that promotes inquisitiveness and bold, even grandiose, initiatives. Focusing on employee strengths and competencies assists movement in this direction.

Needless-to-say, creating the leader of the future will not be an easy task. Leadership behaviors long held sacred will fall by the wayside. The longer these behaviors have been reinforced, the more difficult they will be to change. Future leaders will need assistance in shifting their thinking, behavior and relationship skills so as to be able to motivate and inspire their colleagues, subordinates, constituents, organizations and, ultimately, their industries.

In the case study which follows is an example of a strengths-based OD intervention which was implemented in order to edify a manager's competencies to be most beneficial for an organization's needs. This exemplifies an approach which could be used by an EA practitioner involved in assisting with organizational leadership development.

CASE STUDY #2–THE DEVELOPING LEADER

Following the demise of the executive in the earlier case study, the new corporate management team reconsidered the position. In the position of the previous autocratic executive, another individual, also an engineer, but newer to the organization, was commissioned. He had been very successful in another subsidiary. The senior leadership, recognizing the substantial challenge to this executive in expanding the company, and wanting him to have every opportunity to succeed, supplemented his duties with developmental support. The plan included further education (an Executive MBA) and an executive coach. The coach and the executive worked together for a two-year period. During this time, the executive engaged in assessments of his traits, motivational styles, and strengths. Additionally, perceptions of colleagues regarding his performance strengths, weaknesses and development needs were also garnered. Over the two years, the executive developed insight into his behavior, its origins and he was able to make conscious choices about his actions. Consequently he was better able to appreciate the impact he had on others.

Slowly, but steadily, the executive began changing. He began to experiment and take more risks; while also encouraging such behaviors in others. His style evolved from a heavy handed approach to becoming much more collaborative; thereby, capitalizing on the intellectual energies of his colleagues and subordinates. As a result, a cadre of both progressive and entrepreneurial leaders emerged under his leadership. This team expanded the existing business substantially.

More importantly, their innovation and journeys into new market-places led to new products, new customers and record profits. His ability to capitalize on his own strengths and to leverage the skills of those he worked with provided tangible benefits in terms of increased revenue and profits.

ORGANIZATIONAL DEVELOPMENT AND PRACTICES

EAP practitioners interested in engaging in OD interventions need to understand the many ways in which EAP skills can be used within an organizational context. Historically, the field of organizational development (OD) traces its origin to psychologically related research in the early part of the 20th century. During World War I, Robert M. Yerkes and Arthur S. Otis (both psychologists) developed intellectual assessment instruments for new army recruits. Later known as the Army Alpha and Army Beta these assessments were used to classify recruits for rejection, discharge, assignment or officer training camps. Thus began the first organized effort at candidate selection (Yerkes, 1921).

In the mid-1920s, Elton Mayo and his colleagues conducted studies on the relation of quality and quantity of workplace lighting on employee productivity (Roethlisberger and Dickson, 1939). These studies, conducted at the Western Electric Hawthorne Plant near Chicago, were the first to discover the relationship between environment and productivity. The EAP movement has, as one objective, to increase productivity and can point to the "Hawthorne Studies" as an early influence in understanding the impact of organizational climate on worker productivity.

Group behavior, including team performance and motivation, was studied in national training laboratories during the 1940s. With the expertise of Kurt Lewin, training programs were developed for community leaders. These studies led to sensitivity training and T-Group Models. Further, Lewin studied organizations and developed his model of "unfreezing, changing and refreezing" to understand organizational change (Lewin, 1947). Since these early studies, OD has become well-integrated into organizational and managerial mainstream processes. Today, OD entails a wide range of organizational activities, from the highly technical and statistical (e.g., time motion studies) to the highly interpersonal (process consultation). OD includes involvement in motivation, performance, job design, inter- and intra-group behavior, power and conflict, leadership, decision making, communication, reward systems and organizational design. In virtually every part of an organization in which there are people-related issues, OD has something to offer. Hence, there is a national linkage between EAP and OD interventions.

OD has been described as "an approach to facilitate change in growth," enhancing human skills and resolving difficulties at both the personal and organizational levels (Dorn, 1994). Goals of OD include assisting in efforts of organizational change, enhancing organizational productivity, assessing candidates for position selection, team building initiatives, assisting with organizational culture change; and providing counsel and coaching to senior managers and executives (Beard, 1993). Many OD specialists would also include education and training on psychological or interpersonal issues (e.g., conflict resolution, communication, and so on) as aspects of practice. The common theme among all these practice areas is the application of psychological and behavioral principles, techniques and methods to enhance workplace performance.

The history of EAP is consistent with themes of assisting employees to be optimally productive. In the following section, examples of OD case studies will be offered which can suggest interventions which may be of interest to EA professionals.

CANDIDATE EVALUATION

One of the early, and still primary, uses of the OD consultant is in the selection of candidates for key organizational positions. The selection of candidates runs from the highly assessment-based, which uses subjective, intellectual, personality and even occupational tests, to the process interview in which few or no subjective assessments are used. The evaluation process used depends on the skill and training level of the OD consultant, level of the to-be-filled position within the organization, the comfort level of the OD consultant with inferential data collection and how the OD consultant defines his/her role. The more one's professional definition resides in collecting, summarizing and interpreting external sources of data, the greater the likelihood of using subjective assessment tools for evaluations. The professional who is more comfortable and confident inferring psychological characteristics and intellectual factors from interview data, will be more likely to see him/herself as the primary instrument (Tobias, 1990).

Several critical issues need to be addressed prior to the evaluation of candidates for a position. The understanding of match or fit must begin with a knowledge of the organization as well as the position and the expectations of the candidate. The OD consultant must develop an understanding of the context in which the candidate will work and the demands, characteristics, peculiarities and idiosyncrasies which will contribute to success or failure. Knowing an organization's personality is advantageous to undertaking these assessments. To conduct evaluations without this knowledge is a precarious undertaking.

CASE STUDY #3

The example below illustrates how an OD practitioner participates in candidate evaluation processes. A large Midwestern university was seeking a Dean for its School of Business. While it was not their practice to utilize outside counsel in these matters, one of their search committee members was an alumnus in private business who recommended utilization of an external OD consultant.

Both the university and business school had sterling academic reputations. The position of Dean carried with it both regional and national reputation, as well as financial implications. The previous Dean, now retiring, had been in the position more than ten years and at the university for more than twenty. The search committee was intent on both preserving the fine academic programs they had, while being progressive in an evolutionary manner.

From discussions with the search committee, the OD consultant developed a "Template for Success" as the context. This template was a concentration of those characteristics deemed essential for success within the new position. Characteristics included being democratic but decisive; collaborative but willing to stand up against prevailing thoughts; and, with strong oral presentation skills as well as a progressive leadership style. From these characteristics, as well as position description requirements, in addition to gathering knowledge about university organizational culture, goals and constituencies, the consultant gathered a well-informed context against which to evaluate candidates. From a national search, three candidates emerged as finalists; and each was interviewed by the OD consultant. Data from those interviews were compared to the "template of success" which had been created earlier. The OD consultant then met with the search committee and facilitated a lengthy discussion regarding the candidates. The top candidate was offered, and accepted, the position. Based upon prior agreement, the OD consultant communicated with the nonselected candidates about their match with position needs; this was important feedback for them.

This case study illustrates the principle that, as is true with performance evaluations in general, an incumbent manager's behavior must be evaluated within the context of the organizational culture and its norms regarding values, attitudes and behaviors.

THE FALTERING EXECUTIVE

One area quite familiar to EAP is that of working with employees having performance problems. OD interventions can also address troubled employees; however, within an OD context that person will be a senior manager or executive. With an impaired executive, many persons are affected such as fellow senior managers, subordinates, clients/customers outside the organizations, etc. Because the implications are organizational, assessment data often come from multiple sources. As a result, confidentiality assurances are critical, and complex. The following case study demonstrates an OD intervention in assisting a faltering executive and serves as a comparison with the kind of troubled employee assessments typically undertaken by EA professionals.

CASE STUDY #4–CONSTRUCTING A PLANT MANAGER

The Western Regional Vice President of a large, international construction company was concerned because of several reports he had received about the performance slippage of one his senior plant managers at an important regional operation. After discussing the problems, the VP and the OD consultant decided upon a strengths-based strategy in which to engage the plant manager, so as to alter his faltering performance. As a result, the plant manager was notified of the opportunity to be involved in a developmental project for his own growth and career management. The VP was candid about both the strengths and concerns he saw in the plant manager. With some nudging, the plant manager began to take ownership of the problem and demonstrated willingness to work toward a solution. The plant manager, with the VP, identified several people in the organization familiar enough with the plant manager to provide the OD consultant with information regarding his strengths and weaknesses. The plant manager was also to undergo assessments for the purpose of underscoring his competencies and capabilities, as well as areas warranting change.

The OD consultant interviewed the plant manager and the other recruited employees with open ended, structured interview questions. In addition, the OD consultant asked all participants to fill out a leadership inventory on the plant manager. The OD consultant collected the data and, as previously determined, dialogued with the plant manager himself; and, then included the Vice President in the feedback process. As a result of these discussions, several specific development objectives were identified. The plant manager felt he had a clearer sense of what would be a more appropriate management style and direction; and, as a result he enlisted the Vice President as a coach in helping him move forward. He was so pleased with his process that he also shared the new management direction with his subordinates, and enlisted their help in achieving his goals. Two years post-evaluation, his career continued to blossom. Clearly this OD intervention is similar to EAP assessment and referral in assisting "troubled employees."

EXECUTIVE COACHING

In the past several years, consulting with executives to enhance their management and leadership competence has become increasingly popular; and, some organizations require it for their senior management team. Others use it at specific times in the life cycle of an executive (i.e., when a promotion to new and broader responsibility has taken place). Engaging in the executive coaching process varies on a continuum from being highly behavioral to more insight and process based (Witherspoon and White, 1996). The common denominator in most executive coaching processes is in helping executives change to become more effective, typically during transition periods (Moss and Vogel, 1995). Such interventions usually begin with a data collection phase which involves some kind of evaluation. Often, some kind of holistic assessment is included, involving other executives, subordinates and colleagues. In all cases, objectives are formulated into a developmental plan, which serves as a basis for the coaching experience. The OD consultant then meets with the executive over a specified period of time. Periodically meetings may also include the executive's manager; or, other valued colleagues to help provide additional sources of feedback on the executive's developmental process. In all cases, the focus is on helping the executive in the context of the business objectives of the organization.

In the following example, the OD consultant uses his coaching skills to help a manager learn how to broaden his performance. This type of intervention is not unlike how an EA professional might work with managers wanting to improve their supervisorial skills.

CASE STUDY #5–BRIDGING THE TRANSITION

A manager had recently been promoted to an officer-level position with much greater responsibility and span of control than she previously had held. While having been successful in managing a smaller department, she now had responsibility for an entire functional area. Recognizing both the potential and the challenges, her manager (the President) offered a coaching opportunity to assist in negotiating through the transition period.

The OD consultant was engaged and a consultation project ensued which included an assessment of strengths, motivational styles and behavioral traits. During the evaluation process, the executive's family of origin was discussed and their relational dynamics were elaborated. Parallels were uncovered between her relationship with her father and dynamics she had been experiencing with both subordinates and authority figures. Much of the consultation work was to help the executive develop a level of insight into how her family of origin interactional patterns may have an impact on her current work-related behavior. By doing this, she was able to become more effective in her use of power, authority and role responsibilities.

TEAM BASED CONSULTATION

Organizations often engage OD consultants to assist at a broader level than simply working with the individual unit. With the increased emphasis on fewer layers of management, it is common to see organizational cultures in which intra- and inter-functional teams are empowered to make and implement decisions related to the business. The OD consultant, with both an understanding of individual as well as group dynamics, is uniquely qualified to provide advice, observations of process and communications, conflict and dispute resolution as well as role and rule clarity. Too often, work teams are given empowerment, but little direction. Often leadership is ill-defined, weak or nonexistent. If the responsibilities of these groups are large, there will not be time out for the group to function more adaptively.

The process of group or team-based consultation, as with individual consultation, varies according to consultant. Many OD consultants with training in facilitating groups are highly process-oriented with an emphasis on interaction, *in vivo* conflict and dispute resolution. Others prefer to focus on objective data gathering and use surveys or other instruments, along with the more controlled educational or training emphasis. In either case, the purpose is to form a more functional work group with clear goals and roles, greater cohesiveness and well understood rules of engagement. The organizational team is ultimately responsible for generating business related objectives which must be accomplished for its success.

CASE STUDY #6–TEAM CONSULTATION ONE-BY-ONE

A small, entrepreneurial, high-tech software company had experienced rapid growth which created high levels of stress and often role confusion. As a result, the owner president found himself spending much time resolving disputes and providing direction to a harried, confused and chaotic workplace. Recognizing his skills were more in software development than in management, he engaged the services of an OD consultant to help bring order out of chaos. The project was presented to the wary and somewhat hostile management group. The OD consultant recognized that to be successful, evaluation interviews with key managers were needed. The consultant worked with the president to devise a small set of questions around roles, conflict, relationships and responsibilities. Using these questions, the OD consultant interviewed 10 of the top managers over a two week period. Individual interviews were utilized as opposed to other methods such as surveys or focus groups, in order to develop relationships with managers that would enhance efforts in future coaching initiatives.

As is typical in such situations, common themes began to emerge about people, processes and structure. The rapid growth had created both excitement and insecurity, leading to turf battles, the withholding of information, internal cliques, massive gossip and blaming behaviors. All of these served to take energy away from the business.

Once the data were collected and summarized, the OD consultant met with the president to decide about how to share and utilize the results. They developed a multi-tiered approach to deal with the organizational challenges. Initially, the consultant met with the entire management group to detail the themes which emerged, being careful to safeguard confidentiality and mitigate further blame. Having obtained their consensus about the challenges, the consultant then engaged them in developing smaller consultant-led task groups, along problem identified tasks, to determine solutions over the ensuing months. The consultant met weekly with each small task group to discuss progress in moving toward solutions for the identified problems, as well as meeting weekly with each manager. This individual meeting served to help dissipate negative energy, create a sense of personal ownership and responsibility, focus on positive potential for growth opportunities and to begin working on individual development.

The results were dramatic. At the end of the month, most of the previous problematic behaviors had diminished *even with no further intervention*. Nonetheless, a group meeting was held in which task groups proposed solutions, most of which had already been enacted! The group devised some guidelines for facilitating positive behaviors in the workplace.

This case is an example of how participating in a group process helped to facilitate change. It is complementary to a longstanding EAP interest in facilitating workplace processes that allow organizational members to experience individual and group empowerment.

ORGANIZATIONAL CONSULTATION

Because of the OD consultant's involvement in any or all of the above consulting activities, that person becomes a rich resource and data base of organizational knowledge. By virtue of such immersion, the OD's value to the organization is greater than the time or energy invested simply in helping with projects. By operating in an OD capacity, the practitioner can acquire a sense of the workplace culture and may begin to know where problem areas and hidden opportunities reside. Knowledge of both an organization's structure and employees provides a level of insight which can be extremely valuable to senior management. As a result, the OD consultant is able to provide wise insights and counsel in times of transition, reorganization, restructuring, growth and downsizing. The ability to positively impact the organization multiplies as the OD consultant has time and experience with the organization. This is the highest, best and culminating use of the talent, time and ability of the OD consultant.

Such is also the case for EA practitioners, particularly those who are internal; and, who come to understand through time and exposure, challenges and opportunities which exist at the workplace. In that regard, the effectiveness of the EAP is directly related to the ability to relate effectively, confidently and knowledgeably about organizational issues and at the appropriate managerial level. Consequently, the interpersonal effectiveness of the organizational practitioner may be his/her most important tool.

In order to be of maximum value, the OD consultant must be conversant in the language, ideas, concepts and pragmatics of the work organization. This means learning about the organization's business, i.e., its products, services, marketplace and competition. This naturally gives the consultant enhanced credibility, but it also increases the context through which to understand the human issues of the workplace. While the OD consultant always operates out of a basis of knowledge grounded in human behavior, he/she must additionally demonstrate understanding of the business-related needs of the organization. Otherwise, the OD consultant will be operating in a vacuum and his/her consultation could risk being diminished or trivialized.

To maximize effectiveness, the OD consultant should understand concepts like return on investment (ROI), return on assets (ROA), shareholder value, profit before taxes (PBT), earnings before interest and taxes (EBIT), economic value added (EVA), net operating profit after tax (NOPAT), earnings per share (EPS), time to market, on time delivery, returns, scrap and something about the relationship of the stock price to market and competitive variables.

This is not to say that the OD consultant needs an MBA. It does mean, however, that expanding his/her base of knowledge in business through reading, seminars and experience can only increase the quality and value of the OD consultation. Having elaborated some of the components of the OD practice by way of case example, similarities and differences between EAP and OD will be discussed in the next section.

It is critical to maintain the understanding that problems in organizations ultimately fall on the shoulders of *people*. While an organization's business may be (and usually is) technical, it is the ability to plan, make decisions, solve problems, manage people and process, implement initiatives and communicate that underlies all business activity. It is the fundamental psychological and behavioral characteristics of people and organizations that contribute to business success or failure. Levinson has suggested that all organizations replicate the family structure (Levinson, 1993). At the heart of organizational issues are deep, psychologically rooted dynamics, endemic to individual and family development, such as bonding, guilt, self-image, attachment, structure, dependence, blame and narcissism. All of these common characteristics are well-understood by mental health professionals. It is leveraging this knowledge of human behavior and using it within the context of the business world that allows an organizational consultant to be effective and valuable to the organization. Since EAP professionals are already in that position, they should be valuable as OD consultants.

In terms of the educational background requisite for OD work, generic behavioral sciences information which includes content regarding assessment, treatment planning and intervention methods is the bottom line. An understanding of personality theory, models of therapy, psychological evaluation, human growth and development, individual and family systems, psychopathology, relationship and group processes are all arrows in the EAP quiver. It is this deep and profound psychological, behavioral and interpersonal knowledge which arms the EAP professional in being an effective practitioner/consultant in a typical therapeutic milieu. It is that same body of knowledge which differentiates the EAP professional from other workplace consultants (e.g., management consultants; business consultants) thereby providing a springboard for reaching management with assistance for business related problems.

Therapy and therapeutic interventions are all about some sort of desired change. Whether it is self-image, depression, relationship problems, alcohol and drug usage, weight management, family functioning or conflict resolution, people come to EAP professionals for assistance in moving from unhealthy to healthy behaviors. Whether there is a precipitating event or cumulative stress, the EAP client is seeking a greater level of satisfaction, harmony and sense of positive control.

Similarly, in the business context, it is often around issues of change that the EAP is most valued. Business changes are usually related to individual performance and financial targets. Issues such as growth and expansion, greater competition, consolidation, downsizing and reengineering are all organizational threats which lead to stress and change. These challenges are opportunities whereby EAP consultation can provide great assistance for managing and directing transitional behavior. The multiple changes in the business world, and the speed of those changes, make the need for assistance in creating maximum managerial performance, thinking, behavior and interpersonal skills greater now than ever. A field of opportunity exists at the workplace.

Yet, with the solid psychological and behavioral foundation of the EAP professional, the move to serving as an OD consultant requires some rethinking of the roles and rules of engagement. In the next section, the context and practice skills of OD intervention will be elaborated.

THE PRACTICE CONTEXT OF OD

The shift from EAP professional to OD consultant requires several paradigm shifts and changes in understanding one's role and responsibilities in a business related setting. Businesses are often skeptical and threatened by the presence of psychologically related professionals in their organizations. It is critical that the OD consultant develop credibility with business people by gaining knowledge and understanding of their business targets and outcomes without compromising the role of the behavioral and psychological professional. Fundamental issues such as the location of the consultation activity, one's professional dress and demeanor, understanding business etiquette and vernacular, are all critical changes and shifts in moving from therapist to consultant.

In most therapeutic environments, the treatment is done in the therapist's office. Business consultation, on the other hand, is almost universally done on site at the organization, typically in the office of the consultation recipient. Similarly, the level of formality is typically much greater in the business setting where, even in today's casual atmosphere, suits continue to dominate as standard. The body of knowledge the professional must acquaint him/herself with requires an expansion of exposure to business related issues. The professional would be well advised to begin reading such business related journals as *Forbes, Fortune, The Wall Street Journal, Industry Week*, and *Business Week*. It would also be of value for the EAP professional to consider business related seminars on management and finance to have a basic understanding of business. This is not to say that there is an expectation that the EAP professional become a business person. Rather, it is to say that, as you enter into the business world, one's professional appearance and behavioral credibility are of critical importance in order to be successful as an OD practitioner.

THE FOCUS OF OD PRACTICE

The unit of study in most therapeutic environments is either the individual or the relationship (which could be the couple or family). Even when being involved in a group treatment activity, the individual is the ultimate unit of study. In the business setting, however, it is the norm that multiple relationships will be involved which impact the individual receiving the consultation. The manager, colleagues, subordinates and even customers will often be interviewed as part of a data collection process. They might also become part of an ongoing quasi-consultation group to help the individual continue to increase his/her performance. To expand the thinking of the professional about the unit of study helps move the focus from primarily therapy to consultation.

Issues such as frequency of consultation, length of consultation time and consultation responsiveness also vary in an OD setting. The individuals receiving consultation can be seen as frequently as once a week or as infrequently as once or twice a year. The length of time typically varies from an hour to a half-day, depending on the need for and objectives of the consultation, as well as the data collection process. These are both somewhat different from the standard fifty minute office visit common in EAP practice. Similarly, the OD professional often finds that responsiveness to client needs drives the work, more than complying with a set number of EAP assessment and referral sessions. It is not uncommon, in the midst of a consultation project, for OD clients to call and request additional work and/or information. Thus, the parameters of OD practice vary from traditional EAP assessment and referral. These issues need to be considered as the EAP professional moves into a professional OD assignment.

BUSINESS DEVELOPMENT

Typically in EAP practice, expanding one's practice is done in a traditional manner. It is common for the professional to have business cards and brochures printed and periodic mailers sent to potential referral sources. It is similarly common for the EAP professional to engage in speaking engagements at church or association meetings about psychologically related issues as part of a business development activity. Finally, it is common for individuals in therapeutic settings to make referrals as satisfied customers.

In the OD consultation practice, the manner of developing business is vastly different. It includes first and foremost, face-to-face contact with potential buyers and/or referral sources (Rackham, 1988). While it is possible to get referrals from satisfied customers, it is more likely that the organizational development consultant will generate business through personally meeting with business people and beginning to understand their needs. It is often the case that the OD consultant needs to lead the potential buyer into an understanding of how the services offered by the OD professional can begin to meet his/her needs. While, at times, it happens that typical therapeutic issues such as depression and anxiety drive the business person to call an OD professional, it is less likely than in a private practice setting. Similarly, the projects that the OD professional engages in are larger than the average EAP intervention.

The reference point for the OD professional in terms of self-concept and identification is more that of small business, rather than as a professional in private practice. When you consider the kind of work that is being done, the fee structure that is being applied to that work and the project basis of that work, it is important to begin thinking of yourself as a business person whose main skills are psychological, much as the accounting person thinks of him/herself as a business person whose primary skills are financial. In making this shift in thinking, it is important not to lose your identity as a mental health professional; but, to remember that the context in which you are operating has a business focus rather than a therapeutic one.

ETHICS

It is important to always consider ethical issues as you go forward. As a mental health professional, ethics are well-defined and every mental health profession (i.e., social work, psychology, marriage and family counselors) has a set of ethics to which the professional must adhere. In the business setting, some very fundamental ethical issues need to be addressed.

The first question is always, *Who is the client?* In an EAP environment it is clear that the unit of study is the individual, work colleagues or family members. In a business setting, the client is typically the organization, not the individual (Burke, 1982). It is critical to have a clear understanding of who the client is, going into business related consultation. It is also critical in this regard to understand what outcomes are expected and where the flow of information will be directed. Therefore, an understanding of who the client is, on the front end, is critical.

Related to this is the issue of *confidentiality.* It is the understanding of most OD consultants that information about one's personal life is kept confidential; and is relevant to an OD intervention only to the extent it may portend attitudes and behaviors which could affect one's management style. For example, if a person has been married five times and, in each case, the relationship was an abusive one; or, if one had a history of being controlling or dominating in personal relationships, this history may have workplace implications in terms of one's judgment in hiring and managing other people. Inferences related to this personal history, as it potentially relates to current workplace behaviors, might be the focus of a management consultation. However, under no circumstances would one's personal history be discussed with others at the workplace.

Consequently, it is important before engaging in an OD consultation to have a clear understanding, with the individual, of the rules of confidentiality and how thematic material may be used in order to assist that person's optimal performance. It is critical for the OD consultant to delineate with his/her client how information collected will be used as a part of the OD intervention; including, how it will be analyzed and the way in which results will be shared.

A related and important issue has to do with *boundaries.* In an EA practice setting, boundaries are clearly identified and well defined, in terms of topics such as dual relationships and conflicts of interest. Rigid boundaries exist in order to protect the client and minimize chances for exploitation. In a business setting, however, while boundaries are still important, they may be broader than what exists in EA practice. For example, an EA professional would not have lunch or be involved in social activities with the client. In a business setting, however, it is not uncommon for consultant and client to meet over lunch; or, engage in other business related social activities such as receptions or parties. A good caveat to consider might be for an EA practitioner engaged in OD work to be conservative, maintaining their usual boundaries until it became prudent to do otherwise.

Finally, issues related to practicing outside of one's *area of expertise* are important. The OD consultant who is grounded in behavioral knowledge may acquire business knowledge, but is first and foremost a mental health practitioner. It is important not to stretch one's knowledge to include that of technical or financial matters when one's expertise is not in those areas. This is a temptation which faces the OD consultant, who is often asked about business related issues, whereby he or she has only a nominal understanding. If the consultant wishes to pursue other additional training to include as arrows in his/her quiver, it is important to do this in a formal rather than an informal manner.

As you can tell, operating as an OD consultant is arduous and not to be taken lightly. EA practitioners who have a dim understanding of the difference between their role and that of OD consultant could mismanage their endeavors within a business setting. In this respect, it is important to have a mentor, coach or teacher to help begin negotiating the gap between EA practitioner and OD consultant.

The OD consultant, by virtue of time spent in the organization, develops a good understanding of the organizational culture and the organizational talent. The following case study demonstrates how to leverage that knowledge.

CASE STUDY #7–THE VALUE ADDED CONSULTANT

The OD consultant had been engaged several years earlier to work with the client on a particular, performance related issue. From that single event, the OD consultant had been actively involved with the client on a number of initiatives. During that time, the OD consultant had evaluated every senior level person within the organization, provided coaching for senior management, assisted in faltering executive work and worked with teams which were newly formed or lacking direction. During the course of the work, the consultant had become highly familiar with the kind of business the organization was involved in, including some understanding of the marketplace, the products, the competition and how economic cycles affected the organization. The consultant came to be viewed as a partner in business with the client, while not losing his role as behavioral specialist.

The recent retirement of the president of the organization caused the board of directors to engage the consultant in a two-day retreat to help them understand the organization's future direction. The consultant was engaged as both facilitator with the board of directors as well as providing input about individuals. During the retreat, the consultant was able to knowledgeably discuss the strengths and weaknesses of senior level management in the context of where the board of directors saw the business going. The consultant was able to offer thoughts about, and provoke thinking related to, the current structure as it existed and what might be needed in terms of future leadership direction. At the culmination of the two-days, the board of directors emerged with a new structure and a new management team. The consultant was engaged further to work with the new president and the new management team in order to help them become cohesive as well as to help the president, who was being stretched in his new position, to be optimally effective.

This is the kind of consulting that is the highest and best use of the OD consultant's abilities. It can only happen over time, as the consultant becomes more confident and capable in his/her abilities as well as having gained familiarity with the organization. This example serves to underscore that the shift from EAP professional to OD consultant is not a short journey. However, it is a role where vast opportunity exists and for which an EAP professional may already possess a basic foundation of knowledge about individual, couple, group and organizational behavior.

CONCLUSION

The organizational requirements of the future are clear. To be stellar, an organization will have to be more competitive, have quick service, quality products and perform effectively with fewer resources. The bar has not been raised, it has been thrust several notches higher. As a result, managers have greater responsibility and broader areas of control with less support or training. Clearly, some compensatory measures are needed and organizations increasingly recognize the need for OD assistance. Whether having high level candidates or developing independent work teams, the future for human performance consulting is bigger than ever. With the basic skill set EAP professionals have in the behavioral sciences, many could be well-positioned to move into this growing area of organizational assessment and intervention.

REFERENCES

Beard, M.J. (1993), Organizational development. *EAPA Exchange*, 23, 20-23.

Burke, W.W. (1982), Who is the client? A different perspective. *OD Practitioner*, 20, 1-6.

Dorn, A.A. (1994), Facilitating change: EAPs and the organizational development opportunity. *EAP Digest*, 47, 18-20.

Hamel, G. and Prahalad, C.K. (1994). Competing for the Future. Boston: Harvard Business School Press.

Levinson, H. (1993, August). *Why the Behemoths Fell: Psychological Roots of Corporate Failure.* Unpublished paper presented as the distinguished contributions to psychological practice lecture. American Psychological Association, Toronto.

Lewin, K. (1947). Group decisions and social change. In T. Newcomb and E. Hartely (Eds.) *Social Psychology.* New York: Holt, Rinehart & Winston.

Moss, L. and Vogel, M. (1995, May). Coaching executives in transition. Unpublished paper presented at The Academy of Organizational and Occupational Psychiatry.

Roethlisberger, F. and Dickson, W. (1939). Management and the worker. Cambridge: Harvard University.

Securities Data Company. (1997). Newark, N.J.

Rackham, N. (1988). SPIN Selling. New York: McGraw-Hill.

Tobias, L. (1990). Psychological consultation to management: A clinicians perspective. New York: Brunner/Mazel.

Witherspoon, R. and White, R. (1996). Executive coaching: A continuum of roles. Consulting Psychology Journal, 48, 124-133.

Yerkes, R.M. (Ed.) (1921). Psychological examining in the United States Army. Memoirs of the National Academy of Sciences.

Index

Absenteeism
    dependent care and, 20
    lower among older workers, 55
Abuse, spousal, 87-88
Ageism, 55
AIDS/HIV, 17
Alliance of Work Life Professionals, 41,48-49
Ask the Children (Galinsky), 49-50
Assessment and referral, dependent care and, 23-25
Association of Day Nurseries, 37

Bank of America, 66-67
Boston University *National Survey of EAP and Work/Family Programs,* 43-48
Builders Emporium, 67
Business Week survey, 49

(University of) California, Berkeley, 15-32
Caregivers. *See* Dependent care
Certification, 41. *See also* Professional preparation
Child care movement, 39-40
Clients, challenged as compared with troubled, 4-5
Collaboration, 62-63
Community at the workplace, 9-12
Community Building, 110-112
Computer technology, for older adults, 70-71
Conceptual model for EAP, 1-13. *See also* Emerging trends
Confidentiality, 127,137-138
Consultant practice, for organizational development, 117-140. *See*

also Organizational development
Coping-oriented questions, 8
Corporate culture, downsizing and, 107-108
Corporate downsizing, 89-90,97-115. *See also* Downsizing
Critical incident stress debriefing, 77-94
    applications, 86-91
        departmental reorganization and change, 89-90
        electrocution, 86-87
        homicide-domestic violence, 87-88
        hospital staff suicide, 90-91
        stabbing death, 88-89
    crisis and trauma concepts, 80-81
    future trends, 91-93
    historical development, 78-79
    interventions, 81-82
    process, 82-86
    workplace uses, 86

Days Inn, 67
Demographics
    of aging, 54-55
    dependent care issues and, 15-16
    of workforce and downsizing, 108
Dependent care, 15-32
    assessment and referral sensitive to, 23-25
    definitions, 15-18
    direct service interventions, 25-26
    employee demands and stresses, 19-20
    future of, 30-31
    indirect services, 26-29
    job performance and workplace effects, 20-21

Medical Leave Act of 1993 and, 21-22
presentation of problems, 22-23
professional preparation and, 29-30
scope of problem, 18-19
women as primarily responsible for, 60-61
Dependent Care Assistance Plans (DCAP), 39
Dialogue, 62-63
Downsizing, 60,97-115
  critical incident stress debriefing in, 89-90
  laid-off workers, 99-103
    communication issues, 100-101
    employee counseling, 101-102
    fostering acceptance attitudes, 102-103
    older workers, 102
    support, 101
  organizational issues, 107-112
    altered corporate culture, 107-108
    altered workforce demographics, 108
    collaboration for community building, 111-112
    creating new vision, 109-110
    developing community, 110-111
    performance evaluation, 109
    workplace violence, 112
  principles and background, 97-99
  survivors, 103-107
    cognitive/emotional impact, 104-105
    management issues, 105-106
    typical responses, 103-104

EAP programs
  conceptualization of, 1-3
  managed care and, 5
  number of, 4
  prevalence of concerns, 5
  structure of, 3
Ecologically oriented questions, 6-7

Economic Tax Recovery Act, 39
Education. *See* Professional preparation
Elder care, 15-32,40,60-61. *See also* Dependent care; Older adults
Eli Lilly Company, 50
Emerging trends in EAP, 1-13
  background and principles, 1-4
  community at the workplace as new social contract, 9-12
  ecologically-oriented, strengths-based practice, 4-9
  millenium and, 12
Employee assistance practice. *See also* EAP *entries*
  critical incident stress debriefing and, 77-95
  dependent care and, 15-32
  downsizing and, 97-116
  emerging trends in, 1-13
  older adults and, 53-75
  organizational development and, 117-140
  work/family programs and, 33-52
Employee Assistance Professionals Association, 93
Employee demands and stresses, dependent care and, 19-20
Empowerment, 62
Executive coaching, 128-129

Family and Medical Leave Act of 1993 (FMLA), 21-22,35
Family leave, 15-32. *See also* Dependent care

Gemeinschaft concept, 9-10
Gesellschaft concept, 9
Great Depression, 38

Harvard Business Review, 49
Health care, 57
HMOs, 5. *See also* Managed care

International Critical Incident Stress
Foundation, 93
Interventions, in dependent care
direct service, 25-26
indirect services, 26-29

Job performance, dependent care and,
20-21
Johnson & Johnson Company, 36

Layoffs. *See* Downsizing
Learn-at-lunch lectures, 28
Leisure time management, 71
Eli Lilly Company, 50
Lynch, Dr. Daniel, 48

Managed care, 29
Maslow's Hierarchy of Needs, 67,69
Medical Leave Act of 1993, 21-22
Medicare/Medicaid, 57
Membership, as key concept, 62-63
"Mommy Track," 49

*National Survey of EAP and
Work/Family Programs,*
43-48
New England Telephone, 48

Older adults, 53-75
challenges for older worker, 58-61
non-workplace prevention
interventions, 69-72
computer technology, 70-71
leisure time management, 71
peer counseling, 70
religion and spirituality, 71-72
volunteering, 70
population growth and work status,
54-55

socioeconomic profile of, 55-57
strengths perspective on, 61-72
key concepts of, 62-63
workplace and, 57-58
workplace prevention
interventions, 63-72
case example, 67-69
definitions and concepts, 63-65
post-retirement return to work,
66-67
pre-retirement planning, 65-66
Older Americans Act of 1965, 67
Older employees, downsizing and, 102
Organizational development, 117-140
case studies
candidate evaluation, 126-127
developing leadership, 123-124
leadership development,
123-124
plant manager development,
127-128
rigid leadership style, 119-120
team consultation, 130-132
transition bridging, 129
leadership issues, 120-124
behavioral, 121-122
cognitive, 121
interpersonal, 122-123
practice issues/opportunities,
124-139
business development, 138-139
candidate evaluation, 125-127
ethics, 137-138
executive coaching, 128-129
focus of organizational
development practice,
135-136
organizational consultation,
131-134
poor employee performance,
127-128
professional shift to consultant
status, 134-135
team-based consultation,
129-131
principles and background, 117-119

Organizational downsizing, 97-115.
    See also Downsizing

Peer counseling, for older employrees,
    70
Pensions, 57
Performance evaluation, downsizing
    and, 109
Population, growth of elder, 54-55.
    See also Demographics
PPOs, 5. *See also* Managed care
Pre-retirement planning, 59-60
Prevention/intervention, 63-65
Professional certification, 41
Professional preparation
    dependent care and, 29-30
    for organizational development,
        133

Racism, wage/salary discrimination, 58
Regeneration, 62-63
Religion and spirituality, for older
    adults, 71-72
Retired Senior Volunteer Program, 70
Retirement
    early/involuntary, 60
    non-workplace interventions, 69-72
    phases of, 59-60
    post-retirement return to work, 66-67
    pre-retirement planning, 65-66

Salary/wage discrimination, 57-58
Senior Citizens Right to Work Act, 55
Senior Community Services
        Employment program, 67
Senior Net, 70-71
Sexism
    effect on older women, 56
    salary/wage discrimination, 57-58
Social contract, 9-12
Social Security
    benefit comparisons, 56-57
    earnings limitations, 55

Socioeconomic profile, of older
    workers, 55-57
Solution-focused questions, 7-8
Stigmatization, 47-48
Strengths-based services, for older
    employees, 53-75. *See also*
    Older adults
Strengths-based, solution focused EAP
    programs, 1-13. *See also*
    Emerging trends in EAP
Strengths-based, solution-focused
    questions, 8-9
Stressors, in dependent care, 19-20
Supervisors, education in dependent
    care, 28
Survey of Work Life Initiatives 1998,
    35-36
Suspension of disbelief, 62-63
Synergy, 62-63

Team consultation, 129-131
(The) Time Bind (Hochschild), 49
Training. *See* Professional preparation
Transition bridging, 129

University of California, Berkeley,
    15-32
U.S. Senate Special Commission on
    Aging, 18

Value-added consultancy, 138-139
Violence
    critical incident stress debriefing in,
        87-93
    downsizing and, 112
Volunteering, by older employees, 70

Wage/salary discrimination, 57-58
Wall Street Journal, 47,49
Welfare capitalism, 37
Women, caregiving role of, 60-61
Work, post-retirement return to, 66-67

Work/family policies, 35
Work/family programs, 33-52
  background, 33-34
  current issues, 48-50
  definitions, 35-36
  future prospects, 50-51
  historical development, 37-40
  program similarities and
      differences, 40-43

research on program integration,
      43-48
Working Mother magazine, 49
Workplace, dependent care and, 20-21
Workplace violence, 87-93
  downsizing and, 112
World War II, 37-38

FAX